FOOD COSTING

FOOD COSTING

Amit Sarkar
Awadhesh KumarPal

NAMAN PUBLISHER & DISTRIBUTORS
NEW DELHI

Published by
Sangeeta Jain for Naman Publisher & Distributors
7360-B, Prem Nagar,
Gali No.1, Shakti Nagar,
Delhi-110007
PH: 23823642, MOB.: 09013478302
E-mail: rajivjain72@ymail.com

[The responsibility for the facts stated, conclusions reached etc. is entirely that of the Author. The publisher is not responsible for them, whatsoever.]

Edition – 2022

ISBN–978-81–920935–8-1

SOLE DISTRIBUTOR
JINDAL BOOK SERVICES
LG-4A, Ganpati Bhawan,
4675-B/21, Ansari Road,
Darya Ganj, Delhi - 110002

Jacket Designed by :
S.M. Graphics

Printed by:
Balaji Offset, Delhi-32

Preface

Food cost refers to the menu price of a certain dish in comparison to the cost of the food used to prepare that same dish. In other words, how much you pay for food will determine how much you need to charge for it. Generally, food cost should be around 30-35%. This means that if you pay Rs 100 for something, you need to charge minimum of Rs. 300-350. It may seem like you are charging a lot more than necessary, but keep in mind that you aren't just paying for the food itself but you are paying someone to prepare the food, serve the food, and clean up after the food. Everything in your restaurant/hotel, from payroll to the electric bill needs to be covered by the food costing, you serve.

Food cost has a direct impact on a restaurants' operating profit. Because no two operations are identical, it is necessary to calculate the food cost of your particular restaurant monthly. Industry averages cannot be used as an accurate standard.

The concept of food cost must be examined at several different levels in order to take into account any and all variables. For example, one variable is your menu sales mix. When one menu item sells better than another, there will be variances in your overall food cost and you should know how this affects your profits.

The book contains 11 chapters on Introduction of Food Costing, Basic Cost Concepts, Budgeting and Budgetary Controls, Menu, Menu Engineering, Pricing of Food Products, Liquor Costing, Food Cost Analysis, Standard Purchase Specification, Inventory Controls, Managing Food Revenue and Expense.

This book is designed and presented in an easy to read and easy to understand format. It will be beneficial to both aspiring professionals and those already in the industry.

We hope this text book meets its intended purpose as a practical resource, and serve as a vehicle for promoting the professionalism of this important segment of the Hospitality Industry.

AMIT SARKAR
AWADHESH KUMARPAL

HERITAGE

LEARNING & DEVELOPMENT CENTER

Heritage Learning and Development Centre (HLDC) is an extended arm of Heritage Institute of Hotel & Tourism (HIHT). Heritage Institute of Hotel & Tourism is an Institute of excellence of the upcoming chain of Management Institutes, founded by D. K. Singh, President. At HIHT, our endeavour is to take education to the higher domains of never ending success. Heritage Institute of Hotel & Tourism provides the best possible infrastructure for pursuing best quality Hotel Management Education. HIHT has three campuses Agra, Shimla and Goa and proposed campuses at Kolkata, Pune, and Singapore.

In the modern era, Hospitality Industry is a reality, fighting for extremely challenging phase and getting into a stability mode. There are SMILES everywhere and this is relatively controlled and guarded, a sign of maturing and learning of Hospitality, which is cyclic in nature. The Hospitality Industry reflects a bright future. Earlier days, hospitality was synonymous with only hotel industry, but today this industry holds its important place with tourism. Hospitality academic in India is still in its nascent stage when compared to the west.

HLDC has been developed through the inputs from the industry and experts from the academics. This panel of experts have gone through the book and made suggestions which were incorporated. Every attempt has been made to thoroughly cover the day to day problems faced in the profession. In this field, as in most any other, it is prudent to remember the old adage, actions speak louder than words. The information given in this book makes the students fit for the industry. It provides about technical skills, personality and soft skills and ability to think and make decision.

This book is designed and presented in an easy to read and easy to understand format. It will be beneficial to both aspiring professionals and those already in the industry.

We hope this text book meets its intended purpose as a practical resource, and serve as a vehicle for promoting the professionalism of this important segment of the Hospitality Industry.

Contents

1

Introduction of Food Costing

The usefulness of control information can be increased by establishing standards for each revenue center within the food and beverage operation. For example, instead of computing a standard food cost covering all outlets, a property might establish separate standard cost levels for its coffee shop, dining room, service, and banquet operations. An advantage of this alternative is that each outlet can be evaluated separately based on its own set of anticipated costs.

However, food and beverage managers realise that as a standard becomes more specific, more time is required to develop and monitor it. The longer the time needed to collect information on which to base the standard, or later to measure actual results, the less practical managers may judge the task; and as a result, the less likely they may be to undertake the control activity. In addition, the more complex the development of standard costs becomes, the more likely the task will be met with resistance by those who must collect the information.

Therefore, an ideal control system must strike a balance between the time and effort spent developing the control system and the usefulness of the results the system provides. The principles for establishing standards are the same regardless of whether the property is commercial or institutional, large or small, fast food or gourmet, hotel or restaurant.

Systems for developing food and beverage standards must begin with the menu. The menu should be designed to implement the property's marketing plan as it relates to the food and beverage operation. Because it establishes which food and beverage items will be served, the menu is the most basic and important control tool. Once a menu is created, five standard cost tools can be developed:

Standard Purchase Specifications

A purchase specification is a concise description of the quality, size, weight, count, and other factors needed to describe a desired item. The specified factors should be described in sufficient detail to properly guide the company's suppliers and receiving personnel in the delivery and receipt of the desired products.

Management should establish standard purchase specifications based on menu requirements and the operation's merchandising and pricing policies. Once developed, standard purchase specifications should be given to those responsible for purchasing, the property's suppliers, and receiving personnel. In this way, all of the parties involved in ordering, supplying, and receiving will have the necessary written guides to permit the operation to consistently obtain the quality and kind of food and beverage items desired.

In addition to providing a knowledge of what is required by the operation, standard purchase specifications offer several other advantages:

— Fewer products may be required. Analysing the menu may suggest ways to duplicate product use (use an ingredient for several menu items) so that fewer ingredients have to be purchased.

— Reduced purchase costs are possible if proper quality items are purchased. Developing purchase specifications based on the needs of the menu means that the property will not have to pay a higher price for a product of greater quality than necessary.

— If purchase specifications are properly established, more than one supplier will likely be able to quote prices and compete for the operation's business.

The development of specifications involves time and effort. Time is needed to create the specifications and then to monitor the need for changes as the operation's business evolves. Furthermore, their use will create increased duties for the receiving staff. Finally, since specifications establish the minimum quality expected, over time they may become the maximum quality that will be purchased.

However, considering the many advantages to the use of purchase specifications relative to the few disadvantages, it should be clear they are a critical standard cost control tool. It is only through carefully developed and rigidly enforced specifications that the operation can help assure that the" right" quality product is consistently available for production and service. Remember, however; use of standard purchase specifications will not, alone, guarantee that products of the correct quality will be received unless effective receiving control procedures are in use.

Standard Recipes

A standard recipe is a formula for producing a food or beverage item. It provides a summary of ingredients, the required quantity of each, specific preparation procedures, portion size and portioning equipment, garnish, and any other information necessary to prepare the item. The advantages of standard recipes are equally relevant in both food and beverage preparation. The primary advantage of following a standard recipe is that, regardless of prepares the item, when it is prepared, or to whom it is served, the product will always look, cost, and taste the same. The consistency in operations provided by the standard recipe is at the heart of all control, and many marketing, systems.

There are several other reasons to use standard recipes in addition to the advantages of consistency in appearance, cost, and taste:

— When managers know that the standard recipe will yield a specific number of standard-size portions, it is less likely that too many or too few items will be prepared.

— Since standard recipes indicate needed equipment and required production times, managers can more effectively schedule food production employees and necessary equipment.

— Less supervision is required since standard recipes tell the employees the quantity and preparation method for each item. Guesswork is eliminated; employees need only follow recipe procedures. Of course, managers should routinely evaluate the quality of items produced and ensure that standard recipes are followed correctly.

— If the chef is ill or the bartender doesn't show up, a product can be produced if a standard recipe is available. Granted, inexperienced employees will be slow and may make mistakes. However, if the recipe is in the head of an absent employee instead of on a standard recipe card or available for printout, management will be in an even more awkward position.

Many persons think about the importance of standard recipes for food production; as suggested above, however, they're also critical to control the consistency (quality and cost) of beverages. Today in the U.S. it is critical that standard recipes specifying ingredient and portion sizes of alcoholic beverages be available in consistent use. Liquor liability concerns often arise when standard recipes are not available and or when standard portion controls are not in use. It is always necessary to be able to verify the actual quantity of alcohol (not just number of drinks!) that has been consumed by a guest.

Using a standard recipe does not requite that the recipe be physically in the work area during production times. After a cook prepares a menu item several times, or a bartender mixes a drink several times, he or she will-remember ingredients, quantities, and procedures. It would obviously be impractical if, before preparing a drink, a busy bartender had to refer to a standard recipe. A standard recipe must always be followed and must always be available, but it does not always need to be read.

Developing Standard Recipes

Developing standard recipes does not require throwing out existing recipes and starting over. Rather, it often requires standardizing existing recipes according to a series of steps. Select a time period for standard recipe development. For example, you may choose to standardize three recipes at each weekly cooks' meeting, or spend one hour each week with the head bartender to develop standard beverage recipes. At these meetings, ask the cook or head bartender to talk through the preparation of the item.

Record the recipes in a standard format that will be helpful to those preparing the items. For example:

— Decide on the desirable yield. If 25 portions of a food item are normally prepared for slow periods and 60 portions are needed for busy times, recipes should be designed to yield these servings.

— List all ingredients in the order they are used.

— Decide whether to use weights or measures or both. Weighing is always more precise than measuring, and it is just as practical to weigh liquids, flour, etc., as it is to measure them. Avoid confusion by using consistent abbreviations throughout all the standard recipes you are developing.

— Whenever possible, express all quantities in amounts that are practical for those preparing the item. For example, convert all measures into the largest possible units. Change 4/8 cup to ½ cup, four cups to one quart, or three teaspoons to one tablespoon. At this point you need to be sure that the proper equipment is available. It does little good to specify a three-ounce quantity when an accurate measuring scale is not available. Also, when applicable, recipes should be developed that call for standard-size pans and other equipment.

— Record procedures in detailed, concise, and exact terms. Avoid ambiguous statements. For example, what does" one cup whipping cream" mean? Does it mean one cup of cream that has been whipped or does it mean one cup of cream that must be whipped? When mixing is called for, tell how to mix (by hand or by machine) and provide the exact time and speed if a machine is used. State the size and type of equipment and small wares such as pans or bowls needed and always list exact temperatures, cooking times, and other necessary controls.

— Carefully consider potential sanitation problems which can arise in each step of recipe production; note these and incorporate food handling precautions directly into the recipe. For example, if the operation uses a hollandaise sauce (this sauce is potentially hazardous and is highly susceptible to contamination by microorganisms), a last step in the recipe for hollandaise sauce might state: "Hollandaise sauce is a potentially dangerous food which can become contaminated by microorganisms; always prepare in small batches and do not hold on the serving line for more than one hour."

— Provide directions for portioning. Indicate the type and size of the serving dish. Also, indicate portioning equipment, such as ladle or scoop, and specify the expected number and size of portions. Be sure all required portioning equipment is available for use. If garnishes or sauces are needed, these should be listed.

After the standard recipes have been recorded, share them with other production staff. Solicit their ideas about accuracy and possible refinements. Finally, test the recipes to be certain that they yield products of the desired quantity and quality. After successful testing, the recipe may be considered standardised. Despite the advantages of using standard recipes, there may be some difficulties encountered in implementing them. Cooks or bartenders, for example, may feel that they can no longer be creative in the kitchen or behind the bar. They may resent the need to put things down on paper. Other difficulties may be related to concerns about time. It takes time to standardise existing recipes, and it takes time to train production employees to precisely follow them.

These concerns, however, are minor when compared to the points already noted in favor of using standard recipes. In addition, managers can minimise difficulties with implementing standard recipes by explaining to employees why standard recipes are necessary and by involving them in developing and implementing the recipes.

Standard Yields

The term yield means the net weight or volume of a food item after it has been processed and made ready for sale to the guest. The difference between the raw or "as purchased" (AP) weight and the prepared or "edible portion" (EP) weight is termed a production loss. In general, there are three steps in the production process. The first step is preparation, which includes such activities as meat trimming and vegetable cleaning. The second step is cooking. Holding, the third step includes the portioning of those products that have not been preportioned. A "loss" can occur in any of these steps.

A standard yield results when an item is produced according to established standard production procedures outlined in the standard recipe. They serve as a base against which to compare actual yields. For example, if the standard purchase specifications are adhered to and a meat item is properly trimmed, cooked, and portioned, the actual yield should closely approximate the standard yield.

Determining Standard Yield

Standard yields are determined by conducting a yield test. Ideally, everything that does not have a 100 percent yield should be tested. However, from a practical standpoint, yield tests are typically performed only on high-cost items or on lower-cost products used in large quantities.

The yield from a product depends upon several factors, including the grade, original weight, and preparation and cooking methods. Therefore, it is helpful for a food and beverage purchaser to compare the yields for similar products from different suppliers. It may be possible to substitute a product with a lower cost per unit that provides a yield similar to that of a higher cost product, without compromising the operation's quality standards.

Since the AP weight is already known, the meat must next weighed when it is removed from the oven after cooking. By subtracting the cooked weight from the original weight, you determine the loss in cooking-in this example, an average pounds, 14 ounces per beef rib. Next the fat cap and bones must be removed, and the remaining meat weighed. This edible portion or servable weight-in this example, an average 11 pounds, 3 ounces per beef rib. Subtracting the edible portion (servable) weight from the cooked weight indicates that the in carving and bones averaged 5 pounds, 3 ounces.

Cost per servable pound

Once the edible portion (servable) weight is determined, a per servable pound can be determined. To find the cost per servable pound, first establish the yield percentage. The yield percentage (sometimes called yield factor) is the ratio of servable weight to original weight and is calculated by dividing the servable weight by the original weight (normally both weights are expressed in ounces; there are 16 ounces in one pound), multiplying by 100 to change the decimal to a percentage.

The cost factor

The cost factor is a constant value that may be used to convert new AP prices into a revised cost per servable pound, assuming that the standard purchase specifications; standard recipe, and standard yield remain the same. The cost factor is obtained by dividing the cost per servable pound, calculated as part of the yield test, by the original AP cost per pound. Anytime the AP cost changes from the amount used to calculate the original cost per servable pound in the yield test, a new cost per servable pound can be rapidly computed. This is accomplished by multiplying the cost factor by the new AP price.

Adjusting Standard Recipe Yields

The yield from a standard recipe can be easily increased or decreased by using an adjustment factor. An adjustment factor is found by dividing the desired yield by the original yield. Each recipe ingredient is then multiplied by the adjustment factor to determine the amount needed for the desired yield.

Standard Portion Sizes

Each food and beverage standard recipe indicates a standard portion size. This is the fourth standard cost tool for ensuring consistency in operations. Because a given menu item or drink will be the same size each time it is portioned, no guest will get a larger or smaller portion or a stronger or weaker drink. The benefit is twofold: portion costs for the same food and beverage items will be consistent, and the guest will always receive the same value for the dollars he or she spends. Value is the relationship between price and quality. Basing the selling price of the food or beverage item, at least in part, upon its cost will help to establish a fair selling price, or value, from the guest's perspective.

Assume that an operation does not provide a standard portion size. On one occasion, a guest may receive a very large portion-a great value. Returning at a later time, the same guest may receive a smaller portion at the same selling price-a lesser value and a disappointment for the guest. Consistency, then, in terms of value perceived by guests, is a primary advantage of standard portion sizes. Portion control tools must be available and used every time a recipe or beverage is prepared.

Portion control tools include such items as weighing and measuring equipment, ladles and scoops to portion food, jiggers and shot glasses for beverages, or automated beverage-dispensing equipment. Employees must know about portion sizes in order to follow them. Required portion sizes from each standard recipe should be posted in production areas for cooks and bartenders to refer to. In addition to these lists, some operations use pictures of each item. When these are posted in serving line stations, employees can see how the item should look or how it is placed on the plate.

Standard Portion Costs

After standard recipes and standard portion sizes have been developed, a standard portion cost-the fifth standard cost toolcan be calculated. A standard portion cost is, simply, the cost of preparing and serving one portion of food or one drink item according to the standard recipe. The process of establishing this cost is called precosting.

A standard portion cost is determined by dividing the recipe's total ingredient costs by the number of portions the standard recipe yields. For example, if the cost to prepare a recipe is $75.00 and it yields 50 portions, then the standard portion cost for one item is $1.50 ($75.00 + 50 portions). The prices for ingredients listed in standard recipes can be obtained from current invoices. Today, many operations use computerised precosting systems to keep the per-portion cost of standard recipes current. For example, if the price of ground beef increases, the new cost is entered into the menu management system and all recipe costs in which ground beef is an ingredient are automatically adjusted to reflect the price increase.

Calculating Standard Dinner Costs

Many food service operations combine individual menu items to create dinners or other meals that are casted, priced/ and sold as one selection (although some operations such as cafeterias offer items a la carte-each item individually priced). Because the vegetable varies from day to day (the term du jour for vegetable means of the day, and because guests have choices in the potato, dressing, and juice categories, it would take an impractical amount of time to determine the standard dinner cost for all the different dinner combinations that are possible. For the categories in which the guests have a choice, managers can choose the cost of the most popular item in the category to determine the dinner cost.

For example, if baked potatoes are chosen most often by guests, then the portion cost of baked potatoes might be used when calculating the standard dinner cost. It is also possible to select the item with the highest portion cost in a category and use this when determining the standard dinner cost. In addition, managers can track the actual number of each item chosen for several days, and then calculate an average cost that can be used when determining the standard dinner cost.

Regardless of the method used, planners should be aware of the item cost which is used in calculating the standard dinner cost. Then, when additional items are considered, they can better assure that the per portion cost of the new item will be in line with that used in earlier cost calculations. The worksheet provides four more columns for calculating the standard dinner cost when the standard portion costs of items change (due to a change in an ingredient's price on the item's standard recipe). When this occurs, the new standard portion cost is added to the unchanged costs of the other dinner items to arrive at a revised standard dinner cost. Increasingly, computerised menu management systems are used to update the costs of menu items. These systems are also used to calculate possible food costs when managers consider changing menu prices.

Standard Portion Cost for Beverages

Establishing a standard drink cost for beverages is relatively simple because usually there are few ingredients. Most alcoholic beverages are sold by the liter rather than by the ounce. Therefore, because recipes and bar equipment typically use ounces as a unit of measure, it is usually necessary to convert liters to ounces before making recipe extensions or costing calculations.

Standard cost tools for beverage control

The five standard cost tools-standard purchase specifications, standard recipes, standard yields, standard portion sizes, and standard portion costs-are necessary to establish performance standards for both food and beverages. However, two additional standard cost tools are important to the beverage operation: standard glassware and standard ice size. Standard Glassware. Glassware obviously affects portion size, quality, and perceived value. In too small a glass, highballs made with mixers such as soda, tonic, or water will be too strong since less mixer can be added to the standard portion of liquor.

Conversely, in too large a glass, the drink will taste weak since the greater amount of mixer dilutes the standard portion of liquor. Therefore, the standard drink recipe should specify a standard glass size, which should be determined when the beverage recipe is standardized. A standard glassware review sheet, should be posted in the work area. The same style and size of glass should be used every time the drink is prepared. This means, of course, that sufficient quantities of all necessary glassware must be available at all times.

Glassware is also important in marketing to help carry out an atmosphere theme and to influence the appearance and presentation of the drink. However, while glassware affects presentation (marketing) concerns, it is wise to limit the number of different glasses in inventory. For example, the same glass might be used for ice water, soft drinks, milk, and highballs. If this can be done, problems with the costs of glassware, storage space behind the bar, and training time for bartenders and servers may be reduced.

Standard Ice Size. It is easy to ignore the effect of ice size on drink quality. Although any size ice is suitable for most food service purposes, drink standardisation must consider ice cube size. Bigger cubes leave more empty space in the glass because they do not clump together as smaller cubes do. This space must be filled with something. In a liquor-only drink, such as a martini, the amount of beverage appears smaller, unless a larger portion is served. In a mixed drink, the drink will be diluted by adding more mix. On the other hand, small cubes or shaved ice fill up a glass more completely before a beverage is added, but both melt more quickly. Therefore, a delay in serving or consuming the drink may create a diluted taste. Management must therefore consider its operating procedures to determine the proper size of ice cubes for the operation.

Recipe management software

Recipe management software maintains three of the most important files used by an integrated food service computer system: an ingredient file, a standard recipe file, and a menu item file. Most other management software programs must be able to access data contained within these files to produce special reports for management.

Ingredient file

An ingredient file contains important data about each purchased ingredient. Ingredient file data generally include ingredient code numbers and descriptions, as well as each ingredient's:

— Purchase unit and cost per purchase unit

— Issue unit and cost per issue unit

— Recipe unit and cost per recipe unit

A sample ingredient cost list produced from some of the data contained in an ingredient file. This report is useful for detailing unit expenditures at current costs and monitoring relationships among various product units (such as purchase, issue, and recipe units of the same ingredient). Some ingredient files may specify more than one recipe unit. For example, the recipe unit for bread used for French toast is by the slice; the recipe unit for bread used for stuffing may be by the ounce.

The initial creation of an ingredient file and the subsequent file updates (daily, weekly, monthly, etc.) are often challenging tasks for many food service managers. However, the benefits of an ingredient file often outweigh the cost of creating and maintaining the file. When the ingredient file can be accessed by other management software programs (especially by inventory software), ingredient data can easily be transferred (rather than reinputted) to appropriate management software programs. Since other management software programs rely on data maintained by the ingredient file, it is important that data contained in the file are accurate. If errors are made when initially entering data, all subsequent processing will be unreliable and system reports will be relatively worthless.

Standard recipe file

Computers can assist in generating standard recipes by

simplifying many of the calculations needed. Numerous software programs that calculate recipe quantities based upon estimated unit sales and then print the standard recipe are available. Standard recipe conversion information generated by recipe management software. The software converts recipe ingredient amounts to weights and then to ingredient costs. It can also determine nutritional information for an entire meal (or other period) and define applicable preparation areas.

Some recipe management software programs provide space within standard recipe records for preparation instructions (also referred to as assembly instructions) that are typically found on standard recipe cards. This can be a useful feature when the number of portions yielded by a particular standard recipe has to be expanded or contracted to accommodate forecasted needs. For example, if a standard recipe is designed to yield 100 portions but 530 portions are needed, it may be possible (depending on the particular menu item) to instruct the system to proportionately adjust the ingredient quantities. A recipe for 530 portions can be printed that includes preparation information, thus providing a complete plan for the new recipe's production.

Few restaurants purchase all menu item ingredients in ready-touse or preportioned form. Some ingredients are made on the premises. This means that the ingredients within a standard recipe file may be either inventory items or references to other recipe files. Recipes that are included as ingredients within a standard recipe record are called sub-recipes.

Including sub-recipes as ingredients for a particular standard recipe is called chaining recipes. Chaining recipes enables the food service computer system to maintain a single record for a particular menu item that includes a number of sub-recipes. When ingredient costs change, recipe management software programs must be capable of automatically updating not only the costs of standard recipes, but also the costs of sub-recipes that are used as ingredients in other standard recipes.

Menu item file

A menu item file contains data for all meal periods and menu items sold. Important data maintained by this file may include the menu's identification number, descriptor, recipe code number, selling price, ingredient quantities for inventory reporting, and sales totals (by unit).

This file also stores historical information about the actual number of items sold. Generally, after a meal period, the actual number of menu items served is manually entered into the menu item file, or automatically transferred from an electronic cash register (ECR) or point-of-sale (PaS) system through an interface to the restaurant management system. This data can be accessed by management or by sophisticated forecasting programmes to project future unit sales, determine the number of ingredient quantities to purchase, and schedule needed personnel.

In addition, computer-based sales analysis applications access data in the menu item file to produce various sales analysis reports for management. When menu items, prices, or tax tables need to be changed, the menu item file is accessed and appropriate changes are entered according to procedures indicated in the user's manual provided by the system's vendor.

Actual Sales Records

The information necessary to determine standard food cost may come from actual sales records citing the number of each menu item sold during one or more prior periods. If a sales history has been kept, the total number of each item sold can easily be transferred to the worksheet.

If there is no record of past item sales (for example, if an entirely new menu is introduced), items sold must be tallied daily during the study period. An accurate tally of the number of each a la carte and complete meal item sold during the trial period must be made. The information may come from an analysis of the guest checks created each day during the study period or from a management report generated by most electronic cash registers or point-of-sale systems. The worksheet has space for only 16 days. Because accuracy increases as the number of days increases, two or more forms can be used to tally item sales for at least one month.

By recording this information on a worksheet, total sales (number of units) and total food costs for the trial period can be easily tracked. With this information, an overall food cost percentage can be figured. Because each food item is likely to have a different food cost percentage, calculating the overall food cost involves determining a weighted average food cost. Items with a high food cost raise the average food cost percentage; items with a low food cost reduce it. It is this weighted average food cost that will be used as the standard against which to measure actual food costs.

— The item sales price is the actual selling price of each menu item as printed on the menu.

— Total food revenue represents the total revenue expected from sales of the individual menu items.

— Item food cost is the standard portion cost. If the item is sold individually, this figure can be taken from the pre-casted standard recipe.

— Total food cost is the total cost of all food used to produce the number of items sold.

— The food cost percentage is calculated by dividing the food cost by the sales price and multiplying by 100. The standard food cost percentage for the soup is: While the standard food cost percentage for each individual item is of some interest, one more step is needed to arrive at the overall standard food cost percentage.

— To calculate the standard food cost percentage against which to compare actual food costs, the sum of the total food cost column is divided by the sum of the total food revenue column and multiplied by 100.

The effort needed to calculate an overall standard food cost percentage can be simplified by using one of the many electronic spreadsheet programmes available for a personal computer. The number of each menu item sold can be entered on a daily basis. The computer can calculate total revenue and total costs along with the item's standard food cost percentage and the overall standard food cost percentage.

Standard Costs per Meal

Properties offering more than one menu, such as lunch and dinner, must decide whether to develop standard food costs by meal or across all meals. If by-meal food costs are desired, calculations for each meal must be done on a separate worksheet. There are two advantages to a separate listing. First, when food cost standards are separated by meals, it is easier to compare any differences between standard and actual costs. Second, since corrective action can focus specifically upon the meal period contributing, higher than expected food costs, the reasons for losses can more quickly be identified and brought under control.

There is, however, one serious disadvantage to overcome when standards are established for each separate meal period. To effect control, actual food costs must also be assessed separately for each meal. Even with the use of point-of-sale equipment, the process of determining how much of each food item is used for breakfast, lunch, or dinner is very time-consuming. For example, a manager might know the cost of food that should have been used during a meal period (number of items sold times each item's standard food cost). But if some food was wasted or improperly portioned during preparation, the actual cost of food used would be greater than that determined from the tally of sales. Many food and beverage managers, therefore, find it more helpful to spend time identifying problems common to all meal periods, such as ineffective purchasing, receiving, storing, and issuing, or problems in production and service, rather than searching for problems applicable to a specific meal period.

Standard beverage costs are calculated for exactly the same reason as standard food costs. The manager wants to establish a goal-base of comparison-against which to measure actual results of the beverage operation. The standard beverage cost becomes the goal. The steps in calculating standard beverage costs are:

- Establish all standard cost tools: standard purchase specifications, recipes, yields, portion sizes, portion costs, glassware, and ice.
- Select a time period for the analysis. As with standard food costs, more time and effort spent on determining standard beverage costs will generally produce more accurate cost calculations. However, no system can provide data with 100 percent accuracy. The best time schedule will allow observation of all phases of the beverage operation, including both slow and busy times, or shifts with high, low, and/ or regular prices. At a minimum, the review should cover two or three weeks in succession. Operations with several beverage outlets need a longer observation period for sales to

reflect an average volume and a variety of drinks served.

- Inform all affected staff members-bartenders, food and beverage servers, and others-about the study. They will want to know:
  - The reason for the study-to determine cost expectations for accounting, record keeping, management, and control purposes.
  - Why the study is important-management wants to assess how well the beverage programme is operating.
  - What's in it for them-the results of the study will help staff members know what's expected of them, and cost savings may be shared with the staff.
  - Implications of the study-results of the analysis have no bearing on employment status; no one's honesty or competency is being reviewed or questioned.
  - Procedures for the study-there will be minimal, if any, disruption in on going operations.
- Set rules for the study period, emphasizing that during the trial study employees must very carefully follow all standard procedures. The purpose is to ensure that accurate and reliable information is collected.
  - Standard beverage recipes are to be used whenever drinks are prepared.
  - Portion control tools (shot glasses, jiggers) and standard glassware are to be used in preparing every drink.
  - Management personnel might work behind the bar whenever possible during the study to better assure that required procedures are followed consistently. When not working the bar, managers

should carefully supervise operations to ensure compliance with all standard operating procedures.

  - At the beginning of each shift, the manager should remind personnel that the property is involved in the beverage study and that careful compliance with all procedures is important.
  - Revenue from all drinks served must be collected. Management must approve all complimentary drinks. Personnel must save all drinks returned because of mistakes. Special precautions to minimize the possibility of guest" walkouts" and errors in guest checks should be used.

- Before the study begins, take careful inventory of the quantity of liquor behind the bar.
- Maintain a record of the cost of all liquor issued to the bar during the trial study.
- Record any beverages transferred from the bar and any food transferred to the bar.
- Calculate the standard beverage cost. Close supervision and efficient operations during the study period should yield a reasonably accurate standard beverage cost. That is, with continued use of the standard cost tools, a lower beverage cost percentage most likely could not be achieved without measures such as raising prices, reducing portion sizes, or revising basic operating procedures.

As with the standard food cost percentage, the standard beverage cost percentage is a goal that managers of the beverage operation should work toward. There are, of course, many factors that affect actual practice. For example, errors may occur, control of the beverage operation may gradually become looser, or changes in policy may require revised procedures. These and similar factors reinforce the value of recalling the standard beverage cost percentage when examining actual operating results. The beverage manager should understand that when actual beverage costs exceed standard beverage costs, a problem may exist.

Costing of Dry Herbs and Spices

The Dry Herbs and Spices table uses relatively small measures because these foods are often used in fairly small amounts. The key measures are:

- — Number of tablespoons per ounce
- — Number of ounces per tablespoon
- — Number of ounces that a cup of the item weighs
- — Count per ounce (such as whole bay leaves)
- — Count per tablespoon (such as whole peppercorns)

Costing fresh herbs

Fresh herbs can be used as garnishes of whole leaves or whole leafy stems. They are also used whole in stocks and some roasting recipes. When stemmed and chopped, they find their way into recipes as flavorings and again as garnishes.

Fresh herbs are often sold by the bunch, but it is important to keep in mind that the size of the bunches will vary for one reason or another. One supplier may ship smaller bunches than another, and even if you only buy from one source, the size of a bunch can vary as seasons change. To help you in this regard, the Fresh Herbs table gives you yield information based both on a bunch and on an as-purchased (AP) ounce. To cost whole leaves or volumes of chopped leaves, you first determine the cost of the as-purchased (AP) ounce.

Costing chopped fresh herbs

This was calculated by measuring the number of cups of cleaned, stemmed, and chopped leaf obtained from one bunch. That number was then multiplied by 16 (there are 16 tablespoons in 1 cup), and dividing that result by the AP ounces in the bunch. For curly parsley, the number of chopped tablespoons obtained from 1 AP ounce is shown as 6.62.

Controlling Food Costs

Controlling food costs starts with inventory organisation and control. Over and over we have found that reducing inventory levels and organising food storage areas will significantly reduce food costs. It is a simple axiom: When you have excess and disorganisation you have waste.

Best Guess Inventory/Order System

This system works best when your chef/kitchen manager has been able convince you that ordering is a complex procedure that you the manager/owner should not get involved in. Only someone with his/her many years of experience can understand the obscure secrets of food purchasing. The system works like this:

— In the middle of the lunch hour rush a waitress runs out of crackers. (Side station stocking problem?)

— She rushes to the store room but does not see the crackers because two cases are hidden under other things. (Poor organisation problem?)

— She then rushes to the chef, who is busy on the line, and tells him you are out of crackers.

— The chef was to busy to leave the line and check the storeroom.

— That afternoon whatever salesperson walks in first will get an order for crackers. (Forget price, we need them now!) And because we ran out the chef doubles the order to four cases.

— Now we have six cases of crackers that will sit in the storeroom for who knows how long. (Your money is sitting on a shelf earning nothing)

— Murphy's Law says it is only a matter of time until someone stacks a couple of cases on #10 cans on top of the crackers.

— Chances are good that before you can use up all those crackers, you will have one or more cases of cracker bits and crumbs.

Helpful Hint

In many instances we have eliminated 20% to 50% of the shelves and storage areas to encourage the kitchen to keep their inventory lean and mean. In some cases of extreme overstocking this alone has resulted in reducing food costs by more than 10%.

A rule of thumb we have found to work well is: Order to bring your inventory up to a two order period par level. That is: If you order an item daily, such as produce, order enough to have a two day supply including the inventory you have on hand. If you order dry stores weekly, subtract the inventory you have on hand from what you expect to use over the next two weeks and order the difference.

With this simple concept you should never run out of product, and never have more than a two order period inventory on hand.

Food Storage

Many restaurants still loose product to freezer burn,

contamination and spoilage because of improper storage procedures. Even worse are those restaurants who loose customers because they serve less than fresh meals.

Want to know what improper storage is costing you?

— On the sly, after all your employees have left, take an inventory of everything in your freezer and walk-in that is not properly wrapped, covered or date marked.

— In the next day or two take a second inventory to see how many of these items are still not properly stored. Check for rotation to see if the oldest items are used first.

— Now cost out the items that are still improperly stored. Multiply this by 365 days. Bet that number gets your attention.

— Give your kitchen crew a break by assuming that half of those items will be used up before they spoil. Chances are that even half of your annual spoilage cost will get you thinking what you could do with all that extra money.

Portion Control

Advance preparation can have a critical impact on food costs. Just as you would not stop to drain the swamp when the alligators are nipping at your butt, your cooks will not worry about portion control when deluged with orders during a rush. Advance preparation and portioning not only saves food cost dollars, it also results in a more efficient kitchen, with a more consistent product and faster service to your customers.

Purveyor Shopping

Regularly scheduled requests for bids/quotes from both your current suppliers and new suppliers can loop some more off your food costs. This is an area where you can delegate, up to a point.

— Have one or more of your employees make the calls, using the specifications from your inventory/order form. If a new supplier offers a good price, ask for samples.

— Do not let the employee change your specified supplier on the inventory/order form without your approval.

— Review the price offered and check the quality of the sample before changing purveyors. If you have any doubts, check their service and the consistency of their quality with other restaurants in your area.

— Have a receiving procedure that checks price, quality and quantity at your door. One way is to post your inventory/order form on a clipboard at the back door. The person receiving the delivery certifies that price and quantity of the delivery matches the inventory/order form as well as checking for quality. Exceptions can be noted on the back of the form, and signed by the delivery driver, with management follow-up.

— A double check is to have your bookkeeper check invoiced prices and quantities against quoted prices and amount ordered quantities on the inventory/order form

Lowly Dishwasher

Being the lowest in the pecking order in a restaurant, the dishwasher's potential for profit maximising is often overlooked. More than anyone else he/she can tell you what is coming back from your dining room. How much of your food costs are going into the trash because of excessive portions or just because customers do not like an entree, vegetable or condiment?

Changing a garnish, eliminating a vegetable or reducing a portion may allow you to reduce the menu price, making you more price competitive with the same profit.

The Back Door

The back door is where a good portion your profits can go, if you let it.

— The most obvious step is to keep your back door locked. This will require you to install a door bell outside for deliveries. In addition local fire codes may require an emergency exit bar on the door. Be sure it includes an alarm that must be deactivated by management or designated kitchen personnel before the door can be opened.

— Keep the area outside your back door clean and tidy. As much as is practical you want to eliminate places where stolen food product can be hidden until the thief gets off shift.

— Check your garbage. It is a common trick to wrap a couple steaks up and hide them in the out going garbage. You may also realise considerable saving in lost linen and silverware costs by checking the garbage.

— If you are designing a new kitchen, locate your freezers and walk-ins, where you keep high cost items like meat and seafood, as far from the back door as possible. Make it harder to sneak things out.

How to Make it all Workable

Just like everything else in your restaurant, you are the key to making food cost control work. We favor the two person spot check and prosecute method.

— *The Two person check*—Designate whoever has authority to open the back door to check all garbage before the dishwasher carries it out. If the inspector does his/her job theft will be reduced by requiring two person collusion.

— *The spot check:* This is where management insures the inspector is doing his/her job. This is also where management gets their hands dirty and spot checks the garbage at unexpected times. This clearly establishes you are committed to controlling back door theft. It also validates that you do not ask your employees to do anything you will not do.

— *The prosecution:* You may choose not to go through the hassle of calling the police and actually prosecuting a thief. What you can do is:

  — If your cook/garbage inspector catches a dishwasher taking food out with the garbage, establish that the dishwasher is actually the thief and fire him/her. After a severe reprimand the first time, the same dishwasher caught taking food out again is reasonable proof of his/her guilt in our minds.

  — If you wait outside and find stolen food in the garbage after your cook has inspected the garbage, fire the cook.

  — It is very possible the cook who allows stolen food to go out the door is negligent rather than a thief. No one likes to root through garbage. By firing this cook you will insure that the next cook/ inspector will really check the garbage.

  — Help your cook/inspector. Provide heavy vinyl or rubber gloves and apron for use while inspecting the garbage.

Tricks to Reduce Breakage and Spoilage

— The very first step in breakfast preparation should be to set a supply of eggs out to temper, even before the grill is turned on. Egg yokes are less likely to break if the egg is cracked at room temperature.

— If you use frozen portion cut steaks, layer the steaks in a shallow hotel pan then cover them with clean cooking oil. With this simple procedure:

— The steak's cooler shelf life will be doubled. And, you will have better tasting steaks because the oil prevents the steaks flavorful juices from draining off.

— When broiled the oil seals in the steaks flavor, without leaving any after taste.

— With a longer shelf life you can keep more steaks defrosted, eliminating the need to defrost in a microwave, or attempt to broil a frozen steak if you sell more than expected.

Effective Food Cost Control

It is very important to use clear, properly prepared reports to analyse food cost results. Often, the reports become the focal point due to errors and omissions. Once the report has lost credibility, a meaningful discussion of operational issues is difficult.

A properly prepared food cost report should have a brief summary at the top of the page. Basic operating statistics should be highlighted. We need to know the period of time (week, month, quarter or year) and the ending date. Operating results should include the period sales and purchases, beginning and ending inventory values, food cost and the food cost percentage.

Supporting the summary information, you should include a recap of purchases, inventories and cost of sales by category (e.g. meat, seafood, produce, etc.). Budget comparisons are useful as well if the budgets were thoughtfully prepared. Try to put the current period in context. Show how well the performance was compared to other benchmark periods (e.g. previous month, last year, current year budget, etc.). The comparison section should show in which direction the operation is headed.

Supporting the management summary page, insights and concerns regarding specific components need to be reported. For example, if there was significant waste due to spoilage of produce, the purchasing manager can concentrate on ordering fewer cases (or splitting cases if necessary). Rising prices of gas and corn has impacted the cost of many commodities. Calculate the impact of your meat and dairy price increases on net profits. Bring any other significant findings to management's attention.

Seven Steps to Food Cost Control

1. *Ordering:* The first step is to order right. Having detailed recipes, designing purchasing specifications, doing comparative shopping based on those specifications, and comparing quality, price and service, etc. Oh yes, don't order too early in order to avoid spoilage, wasted storage space and lost interest on your money. Don't order too late, so premium costs and delivery charges accrue.
2. *Receiving:* The fundamentals are obvious: count; weigh; inspect for condition and quality; verify against the purchase order; keep the receiving area clean and uncluttered; limit access to the receiving area; train the person receiving and make him or her responsible. Get credit memos from the delivery driver.
3. *Storing:* Is the method and place of storage for the various items appropriate for the item? Is it secure from pilferage? Are the shelves strong enough for the

product, allow air circulation and easy to clean? Are all items stored at a temperature appropriate for that product? Are items dated (with year, in some cases) and priced? Is the storage area orderly and clean? Should shelves be labeled and maybe even stocking quantities noted?

4. *Issuing:* What is issuing based on? Who has access and or authority to issue or take things from the secured store rooms and walk-ins? Are issues being made in appropriate quantities and at appropriate times? Is there a relationship to volume or reasonable par stocks? Are issues being accounted for? Is a perpetual inventory or sign out sheet designed specifically for your operation or a particular store room in use?
5. *Preparation:* Phrases that come to mind include: trim properly; use trimmings for stock pots and other recipes. Proper tools, sharp knives, clean and neat working area, enforcing a policy of following recipes, and having photos of finished products available and used regularly are also critical.
6. *Cooking:* Proper temperatures, proper cooking times, following recipes carefully, using photographs of finished products, correct size, material, and type of utensils and cookware, clean work area.
7. *Serving:* Serving is not only about portion control, it is also about decisions made regarding portion size and presentation. With a buffet, it is obvious. Proper serving utensils, proper holding/serving equipment, right presentation order, plate sizes, etc. In a bar its easy, too. Jiggers or other measuring and control devices and very strict discipline. Dining room service should be easy to control using good kitchen supervisors, trained cooks, photographs for both cooks and servers, etc. Watch what comes back from bused tables to see if portions are proper. Marketing

decisions may drive large portions but if the patrons are not eating it or taking it home, the portion size or the recipe should be reconsidered. Proper china for each item served is important for both presentation and portion control.

Work hard on your cost controls and be consistent about them. One element of controlling food cost covers all seven categories: thorough training. Give your staff the ability and knowledge and confidence to do their jobs properly and to your specifications. Inconsistency and failure to enforce procedures will drive costs skyward. Failure here is like throwing money away.

99 Sins of Food Cost Control

1. Order not correctly checked in due to either incompetent person or inattentiveness.
2. Due to the lack of food security (locked back door), food pilfered by employees or service personnel.
3. Frozen food not rotated causing old foods in the storage areas to freezer burn.
4. Freezer door not correctly closed allowing warm air to prematurely thaw food. Also, unlocked door, causing the high possibility of theft of goods.
5. Dry foods stored directly on floor, subject to being spoiled by mop water and vermin infestation.
6. Dirty corner causing roaches or rats nest which feed on food products.
7. Torn bag of breading, flour, or sugar in stockroom.
8. Chemicals stored next to food causing possible spoilage and consumer poisoning.
9. Dry foods shelved haphazardly resulting in probable over-ordering due to incorrect inventory, possible unknown pilfering, and poor cost reporting.

10. Frozen foods not categorically shelved causing incorrect inventory (over ordering), poor cost reporting, and possible unknown pilfering.
11. Perishable items (e.g. oysters, chicken) not iced down periodically, speeding spoilage.
12. Over-inventory of salad dressing creamers causing crushed, spoiled product.
13. Opened containers of salad back-ups causing distasteful odors and spoilage of salad backup foods.
14. Opened containers of prepared mixes and food allowing speed up of spoilage because of air flow.
15. Frozen products stored too close together not allowing flow of freezing air, and creating warm air pockets where frozen food thaws and spoils.
16. Rusty or dirty shelf which creates filthy particles falling into foods and causing spoilage.
17. Cooler doors not sealed or correctly closed allowing warm air to enter cooler(s) and keeping temperatures well above a safe level of 33 to 38 degrees.
18. Storeroom door not locked.
19. Manager always in office waging paperwork battle with costs and not aware of problems which actually cause these costs.
20. Poor order book maintenance and system of recording invoices and purchases.
21. Poor record of fryer, grill, and oven maintenance causing equipment not to operate properly.
22. Poor, inaccurate kitchen production sheets which cause waste and spoilage which allow over production and waste.
23. Deep fryer fat not skimmed and filtered of foreign floating food particles, thus accelerating shortening breakdown.

24. Poorly trained cook putting too much food into fryer, splashing basket around, thus speeding shortening breakdown.
25. Cook not shaking excess oil before depositing hot foods into holding trays.
26. Too much frozen or prepped food on shelves in line reach-in.
27. Fryer, oven, and grill temperatures not regularly calibrated.
28. Poorly trained cook splashing water into shortening fryers causing shortening breakdown.
29. Too many fryers, grills, or ovens on for normal business causing wasteful energy consumption.
30. Too many opened bags of French fries in reach in freezer causing particles strewn on freezer floor and ice particles on product.
31. Cook over-cooking for production needs.
32. Cook over-cooking fry baskets, resulting in spilled, unusable product when transferring food from fryer to warmer pan
33. Cook person allowed to eat cooked foods while on duty.
34. Cook burning meats on grill because of inattentiveness.
35. Cook over-cooking food in microwave.
36. Sauté cook having too much thawed, uniced product on table.
37. Kitchen Manager or chef having too much breaded product or prepped sautés for business.
38. Management allowing employees to come and go with cooked foods and drinks without proper eat-check-control.

39. Part-time employees dispensing inaccurate portions.
40. Linemen not weighing portions.
41. Kitchen employees eating customers food.
42. Food production workers mishandling hot food and dropping too much on floor.
43. Cold drinks on top of production line spilling and spoiling cooked foods.
44. Linemen mishandling and crushing cooked foods.
45. Production People filling plates faster than wait staff can pick up orders, thus causing cold food servings to customers.
46. Wait staff over stating order and having customer reorder requests.
47. Wait staff over garnishing plates.
48. Wait staff taking more margarine or butter pats than requested or not asking if customer wants margarine.
49. Wait staff making super salad out of two normal sized salads.
50. Wait staff taking five salad dressings to one table.
51. Wait staff nibbling customers food while waiting for reorder.
52. Members of wait staff discounting friend's meal tickets.
53. Wait staff or hostess guessing prices because no list is posted on special orders at the cash register station.
54. Kitchen employees not scraping remaining slaw or tartar sauce from "empty" container with a rubber tipped scraper.
55. Manager still procrastinating in office over high costs and never checking things in the production/ consumption areas of the restaurant.

56. Kitchen manager not prepping enough salads, therefore forcing wait staff into walk-in cooler to sloppily prepare salads.
57. Wait staff having to make their own salad and spill too much because they are in a hurry.
58. Wait staff not scraping ketchup cans with a spatula as they fill the bottles.
59. Kitchen help spoiling frozen food by quick thawing same under hot water.
60. Prep worker filling sink with raw seafood next to sink full of soapy water.
61. Breaded fish not immediately stored in cooler causing product to quickly spoil or get mushy.
62. Prep worker not preparing food according to standards established by chef or kitchen manager.
63. Large cutting and mix machines not scraped of excess mix.
64. Food production employees not using standard recipes approved by management or chef.
65. Kitchen manager hurriedly preparing breaded food and litters floor with breading.
66. Reach-in- freezer not locked or is holding unrotated food.
67. Hungry kitchen worker eating one salad while prepping five.
68. Wait staff emptying good hot coffee out of pot into disposal sink
69. Kitchen workers wiping up spills with paper or cloth napkins because manager believes it's cost effective to reduce bar towel rentals.
70. Bus person discarding unopened salad dressings or creamers which could be recycled.

71. Dishwasher improperly using dishwasher chemicals.
72. Dishwasher not measuring presoak for silverware.
73. Dishwasher adding rinse dry to machine manually.
74. Food prep worker adding 1/2 gallon or more buttermilk to hushpuppy mix.
75. Wait staff leaving beer tap on.
76. Wait staff drawing beer incorrectly leaving three 1/2 glasses of foam to every glass drawn.
77. Wait staff taking pitchers of soft drinks to customers and not charging them correctly.
78. Wait staff munching crackers or rolls and drinking Pepsi or beer while on duty or off duty.
79. Soup pots not being rotated or refilled and being allowed to burn up.
80. Kitchen worker preparing too much sweet tea for normal business.
81. Wait staff cleaning spill with napkins rather than bar towels.
82. Wait staff discarding pitcher of tea into sink rather than recycling.
83. Wait staff brewing a larger urn of coffee at ten minutes to closing rather than a small pot.
84. Iced tea brewers spilled all over counter and wetting one full bus pan of wrapped silverware because of leaky tea dispenser valve or wait staff leaving valve open.
85. Hundreds of wrapped straws ruined because wait staff, while drinking their soda, horseplay's with bus person and spills their drink into the straw box.
86. On-duty bus person munching French fries and soda.
87. Pan of breaded raw food placed on top of ice machine at lunch, forgotten, and quickly spoiled by the machines heat.

88. Improper control of employee meals because manager is still in office pondering the mysteries of high food expenses.
89. Three on-duty night employees are having three course meals after rush without eat-checks.
90. Work staff filling glasses with gratis soft drinks through out the day; ten half drunk Pepsis are consumed by one employee during his/her two- hour tour of duty, throwing half of each away.
91. Wait staff tray of prepared food knocked off service area counter because it is set down in a busy traffic area.
92. No control on numbered guest tickets; consequently, wait staff ring up and discard tickets for friends meals.
93. Untrained hostess gives gratis on a $75 ticket because of a minor $2 complaint.
94. Restaurant staff and manager's assistant freely consume after dinner mints without paying for them.
95. Closing waiter leaves container of creamers out overnight.
96. Night clean-up crew uses too much cleaning solution to clean up a small area.
97. Night crew accidentally leaves 8 lbs. of lobster tails in sink overnight.
98. Manager still philosophising, rationalising his high food costs in the office.
99. Not letting your Pocahontas Distributor DSR help you contain those costs!

2

Basic Cost Concepts

Cost techniques have a precedence over the other techniques since accounting treatment of cost is often both complex and financially significant. Cost accounting was merely considered to be a technique for the ascertainment of costs of products or services on the basis of historical data. In course of time, due to competitive nature of the market, it was realised that ascertaining of cost is not so important as controlling costs. Hence, cost accounting started to be considered more as a technique for cost control as compared to cost ascertainment.

Due to the technological developments in all fields, cost reduction has also come within the ambit of cost accounting. Cost accounting is, thus, concerned with recording, classifying and summarising costs for determination of costs of products or services, planning, controlling and reducing such costs and furnishing of information to management for decision making. According to Charles T. Horngren, cost accounting is a quantitative method that accumulates, classifies, summarises and interprets information for the following three major purposes:

— Operational planning and control

— Special decisions

— Product decisions

Cost accounting, thus, provides various information to management for all sorts of decisions. It serves multiple purposes on account of which it is generally indistinguishable from management accounting or so-called internal accounting. Wilmot has summarised the nature of cost accounting as "the analysing, recording, standardising, forecasting, comparing, reporting and recommending" and the role of a cost accountant as "a historian, news agent and prophet." As a historian, he should be meticulously accurate and sedulously impartial. As a news agent, he should be up to date, selective and pithy. As a prophet, he should combine knowledge and experience with foresight and courage.

Concept of Cost

Cost accounting is concerned with cost and therefore is necessary to understand the meaning of term cost in a proper perspective. In general, cost means the amount of expenditure (actual or notional) incurred on, or attributable to a given thing. However, the term cost cannot be exactly defined. Its interpretation depends upon the following factors:

— The nature of business or industry

— The context in which it is used

In a business where selling and distribution expenses are quite nominal the cost of an article may be calculated without considering the selling and distribution overheads. At the same time, in a business where the nature of a product requires heavy selling and distribution expenses, the calculation of cost without taking into account the selling and distribution expenses may prove very costly to a business. The cost may be factory cost, office cost, cost of sales and even an item of expense. For example, prime cost includes expenditure on direct materials, direct labour and direct expenses. Money spent on materials is termed as cost of materials just like money spent on labour is called cost of labour and so on. Thus, the use of term cost without understanding the circumstances can be misleading.

Different costs are found for different purposes. The work-in-progress is valued at factory cost while stock of finished goods is valued at office cost. Numerous other examples can be given to show that the term "cost" does not mean the same thing under all circumstances and for all purposes. Many items of cost of production are handled in an optional manner which may give different costs for the same product or job without going against the accepted principles of cost accounting. Depreciation is one of such items. Its amount varies in accordance with the method of depreciation being used. However, endeavor should be, as far as possible, to obtain an accurate cost of a product or service.

Elements of Cost

Following are the three broad elements of cost:

Material

The substance from which a product is made is known as material. It may be in a raw or a manufactured state. It can be direct as well as indirect.

Direct material

The material which becomes an integral part of a finished product and which can be conveniently assigned to specific physical unit is termed as direct material. Following are some of the examples of direct material:

— All material or components specifically purchased, produced or requisitioned from stores

— Primary packing material (e.g., carton, wrapping, cardboard, boxes etc.)

— Purchased or partly produced components

Direct material is also described as process material, prime cost material, production material, stores material, constructional material etc.

Indirect Material

The material which is used for purposes ancillary to the business and which cannot be conveniently assigned to specific physical units is termed as indirect material. Consumable stores, oil and waste, printing and stationery material etc. are some of the examples of indirect material. Indirect material may be used in the factory, office or the selling and distribution divisions.

Labour

For conversion of materials into finished goods, human effort is needed and such human effort is called labour. Labour can be direct as well as indirect.

Direct labour

The labour which actively and directly takes part in the production of a particular commodity is called direct labour. Direct labour costs are, therefore, specifically and conveniently traceable to specific products. Direct labour can also be described as process labour, productive labour, operating labour, etc.

Indirect labour

The labour employed for the purpose of carrying out tasks incidental to goods produced or services provided, is indirect labour. Such labour does not alter the construction, composition or condition of the product. It cannot be practically traced to specific units of output. Wages of storekeepers, foremen, timekeepers, directors' fees, salaries of salesmen etc, are examples of indirect labour costs. Indirect labour may relate to the factory, the office or the selling and distribution divisions.

Expenses

Expenses may be direct or indirect.

Direct expenses

These are the expenses that can be directly, conveniently and wholly allocated to specific cost centers or cost units. Examples of such expenses are as follows:

— Hire of some special machinery required for a particular contract

— Cost of defective work incurred in connection with a particular job or contract etc.

Direct expenses are sometimes also described as chargeable expenses.

Indirect expenses

These are the expenses that cannot be directly, conveniently and wholly allocated to cost centers or cost units. Examples of such expenses are rent, lighting, insurance charges etc.

Overhead

The term overhead includes indirect material, indirect labour and indirect expenses. Thus, all indirect costs are overheads.

A manufacturing organisation can broadly be divided into the following three divisions:

— Factory or works, where production is done

— Office and administration, where routine as well as policy matters are decided

— Selling and distribution, where products are sold and finally dispatched to customers

Overheads may be incurred in a factory or office or selling and distribution divisions. Thus, overheads may be of three types:

Factory overheads

They include the following things:

— Indirect material used in a factory such as lubricants, oil, consumable stores etc.

— Indirect labour such as gatekeeper, timekeeper, works manager's salary etc.

— Indirect expenses such as factory rent, factory insurance, factory lighting etc.

Office and administration overheads

They include the following things:

— Indirect materials used in an office such as printing and stationery material, brooms and dusters etc.

— Indirect labour such as salaries payable to office manager, office accountant, clerks, etc.

— Indirect expenses such as rent, insurance, lighting of the office

Selling and distribution overheads

They include the following things:

- Indirect materials used such as packing material, printing and stationery material etc.
- Indirect labour such as salaries of salesmen and sales manager etc.
- Indirect expenses such as rent, insurance, advertising expenses etc.

Elements of Cost

- Direct material
- Direct labour
- Direct expenses
- Overheads
- Factory overheads
- Selling and distribution overheads
- Office and administration overheads
- Indirect material
- Indirect labour
- Indirect expenses
- Indirect material
- Indirect labour
- Indirect expenses
- Indirect material
- Indirect labour
- Indirect expenses

Components of Total Cost

Prime cost

Prime cost consists of costs of direct materials, direct labours and direct expenses. It is also known as basic, first or flat cost.

Factory cost

Factory cost comprises prime cost and, in addition, works or factory overheads that include costs of indirect materials, indirect labours and indirect expenses incurred in a factory. It is also known as works cost, production or manufacturing cost.

Office cost

Office cost is the sum of office and administration overheads and factory cost. This is also termed as administration cost or the total cost of production.

Total cost

Selling and distribution overheads are added to the total cost of production to get total cost or the cost of sales.

Cost Sheet

Cost sheet is a document that provides for the assembly of an estimated detailed cost in respect of cost centers and cost units. It analyses and classifies in a tabular form the expenses on different items for a particular period. Additional columns may also be provided to show the cost of a particular unit pertaining to each item of expenditure and the total per unit cost.

Cost sheet may be prepared on the basis of actual data (historical cost sheet) or on the basis of estimated data (estimated cost sheet), depending on the technique employed and the purpose to be achieved. The techniques of preparing a cost sheet can be understood with the help of the following examples.

Classification of Cost

Cost may be classified into different categories depending

upon the purpose of classification. Some of the important categories in which the costs are classified are as follows:

1. Fixed, variable and semi-variable costs

The cost which varies directly in proportion with every increase or decrease in the volume of output or production is known as variable cost. Some of its examples are as follows:

— Wages of labourers

— Cost of direct material

— Power

The cost which does not vary but remains constant within a given period of time and a range of activity inspite of the fluctuations in production is known as fixed cost. Some of its examples are as follows:

— Rent or rates

— Insurance charges

— Management salary

The cost which does not vary proportionately but simultaneously does not remain stationary at all times is known as semi-variable cost. It can also be named as semi-fixed cost. Some of its examples are as follows:

— Depreciation

— Repairs

Fixed costs are sometimes referred to as "period costs" and variable costs as "direct costs" in system of direct costing. Fixed costs can be further classified into:

— Committed fixed costs

— Discretionary fixed costs

Committed fixed costs consist largely of those fixed costs that arise from the possession of plant, equipment and a basic organisation structure. For example, once a building is erected and a plant is installed, nothing much can be done to reduce the costs such as depreciation, property taxes, insurance and salaries of the key personnel etc. without impairing an organisation's competence to meet the long-term goals.

Discretionary fixed costs are those which are set at fixed amount for specific time periods by the management in budgeting process. These costs directly reflect the top management policies and have no particular relationship with volume of output. These costs can, therefore, be reduced or entirely eliminated as demanded by the circumstances. Examples of such costs are research and development costs, advertising and sales promotion costs, donations, management consulting fees etc. These costs are also termed as managed or programmed costs.

In some circumstances, variable costs are classified into the following:

— Discretionary cost

— Engineered cost

The term discretionary costs is generally linked with the class of fixed cost. However, in the circumstances where management has predetermined that the organisation would spend a certain percentage of its sales for the items like research, donations, sales promotion etc., discretionary costs will be of a variable character. Engineered variable costs are those variable costs which are directly related to the production or sales level. These costs exist in those circumstances where specific relationship exists between input and output. For example, in an automobile industry there may be exact specifications as one radiator, two fan belts, one battery etc. would be required for one car. In a case where more than one car is to be produced, various inputs will have to be increased in the direct proportion of the output.

Thus, an increase in discretionary variable costs is due to the authorisation of management whereas an increase in engineered variable costs is due to the volume of output or sales.

2. Product costs and period costs

The costs which are a part of the cost of a product rather than an expense of the period in which they are incurred are called as "product costs." They are included in inventory values. In financial statements, such costs are treated as assets until the goods they are assigned to are sold. They become an expense at that time. These costs may be fixed as well as variable, e.g., cost of raw materials and direct wages, depreciation on plant and equipment etc.

The costs which are not associated with production are called period costs. They are treated as an expense of the period in which they are incurred. They may also be fixed as well as variable. Such costs include general administration costs, salaries salesmen and commission, depreciation on office facilities etc. They are charged against the revenue of the relevant period. Differences between opinions exist regarding whether certain costs should be considered as product or period costs. Some accountants feel that fixed manufacturing costs are more closely related to the passage of time than to the manufacturing of a product. Thus, according to them variable manufacturing costs are product costs whereas fixed manufacturing and other costs are period costs. However, their view does not seem to have been yet widely accepted.

3. Direct and indirect costs

The expenses incurred on material and labour which are economically and easily traceable for a product, service or job are considered as direct costs. In the process of manufacturing of production of articles, materials are purchased, labourers are employed and the wages are paid to them. Certain other expenses are also incurred directly. All of these take an active and direct part in the manufacture of a particular commodity and hence are called direct costs.

The expenses incurred on those items which are not directly chargeable to production are known as indirect costs. For example, salaries of timekeepers, storekeepers and foremen. Also certain expenses incurred for running the administration are the indirect costs. All of these cannot be conveniently allocated to production and hence are called indirect costs.

4. Decision-making costs and accounting costs

Decision-making costs are special purpose costs that are applicable only in the situation in which they are compiled. They have no universal application. They need not tie into routine-financial accounts. They do not and should not conform the accounting rules. Accounting costs are compiled primarily from financial statements. They have to be altered before they can be used for decision-making. Moreover, they are historical costs and show what has happened under an existing set of circumstances. Decision-making costs are future costs. They represent what is expected to happen under an assumed set of conditions. For example, accounting costs may show the cost of a product when the operations are manual whereas decision-making cost might be calculated to show the costs when the operations are mechanised.

5. Relevant and irrelevant costs

Relevant costs are those which change by managerial decision. Irrelevant costs are those which do not get affected by the decision. For example, if a manufacturer is planning to close down an unprofitable retail sales shop, this will affect the wages payable to the workers of a shop. This is relevant in this connection since they will disappear on closing down of a shop. But prepaid rent of a shop or unrecovered costs of any equipment which will have to be scrapped are irrelevant costs which should be ignored.

6. Shutdown and sunk costs

A manufacturer or an organisation may have to suspend its operations for a period on account of some temporary difficulties, e.g., shortage of raw material, non-availability of requisite labour etc. During this period, though no work is done yet certain fixed costs, such as rent and insurance of buildings, depreciation, maintenance etc., for the entire plant will have to be incurred. Such costs of the idle plant are known as shutdown costs.

Sunk costs are historical or past costs. These are the costs which have been created by a decision that was made in the past and cannot be changed by any decision that will be made in the future. Investments in plant and machinery, buildings etc. are prime examples of such costs. Since sunk costs cannot be altered by decisions made at the later stage, they are irrelevant for decision-making.

An individual may regret for purchasing or constructing an asset but this action could not be avoided by taking any subsequent action. Of course, an asset can be sold and the cost of the asset will be matched against the proceeds from sale of the asset for the purpose of determining gain or loss. The person may decide to continue to own the asset. In this case, the cost of asset will be matched against the revenue realised over its effective life. However, he/she cannot avoid the cost which has already been incurred by him/her for the acquisition of the asset. It is, as a matter of fact, sunk cost for all present and future decisions.

7. Controllable and uncontrollable costs

Controllable costs are those costs which can be influenced by the ratio or a specified member of the undertaking. The costs that cannot be influenced like this are termed as uncontrollable costs. A factory is usually divided into a number of responsibility centers, each of which is in charge of a specific level of management. The officer incharge of a particular department can control costs only of those matte$ which come directly under his control, not of other matte$. For example, the expenditure incurred by tool room is controlled by the foreman incharge of that section but the share of the tool room expenditure which is apportioned to a machine shop cannot be controlled by the foreman of that shop. Thus, the difference between controllable and uncontrollable costs is only in relation to a particular individual or level of management. The expenditure which is controllable by an individual may be uncontrollable by another individual.

8. Avoidable or escapable costs and unavoidable or inescapable costs

Avoidable costs are those which will be eliminated if a segment of a business (e.g., a product or department) with which they are directly related is discontinued. Unavoidable costs are those which will not be eliminated with the segment. Such costs are merely reallocated if the segment is discontinued. For example, in case a product is discontinued, the salary of a factory manager or factory rent cannot be eliminated. It will simply mean that certain other products will have to absorb a large amount of such overheads. However, the salary of people attached to a product or the bad debts traceable to a product would be eliminated. Certain costs are partly avoidable and partly unavoidable. For example, closing of one department of a store might result in decrease in delivery expenses but not in their altogether elimination. It is to be noted that only avoidable costs are relevant for deciding whether to continue or eliminate a segment of a business.

9. Imputed or hypothetical costs

These are the costs which do not involve cash outlay. They are not included in cost accounts but are important for taking into consideration while making management decisions. For example, interest on capital is ignored in cost accounts though it is considered in financial accounts. In case two projects require unequal outlays of cash, the management should take into consideration the capital to judge the relative profitability of the projects.

10. Differentials, incremental or decrement cost

The difference in total cost between two alternatives is termed as differential cost. In case the choice of an alternative results in an increase in total cost, such increased costs are known as incremental costs. While assessing the profitability of a proposed change, the incremental costs are matched with incremental revenue.

11. Out-of-pocket costs

Out-of-pocket cost means the present or future cash expenditure regarding a certain decision that will vary depending upon the nature of the decision made. For example, a company has its own trucks for transporting raw materials and finished products from one place to another. It seeks to replace these trucks by keeping public carriers. In making this decision, of course, the depreciation of the trucks is not to be considered but the management should take into account the present expenditure on fuel, salary to drive$ and maintenance. Such costs are termed as out-of-pocket costs.

12. Opportunity cost

Opportunity cost refers to an advantage in measurable terms that have foregone on account of not using the facilities in the manner originally planned. For example, if a building is proposed to be utilised for housing a new project plant, the likely revenue which the building could fetch, if rented out, is the opportunity cost which should be taken into account while evaluating the profitability of the project.

13. Traceable, untraceable or common costs

The costs that can be easily identified with a department, process or product are termed as traceable costs. For example, the cost of direct material, direct labour etc. The costs that cannot be identified so are termed as untraceable or common costs. In other words, common costs are the costs incurred collectively for a number of cost centers and are to be suitably apportioned for determining the cost of individual cost centers. For example, overheads incurred for a factory as a whole, combined purchase cost for purchasing several materials in one consignment etc.

Joint cost is a kind of common cost. When two or more products are produced out of one material or process, the cost of such material or process is called joint cost. For example, when cottonseeds and cotton fibers are produced from the same material, the cost incurred till the split-off or separation point will be joint costs.

14. Production, administration and selling and distribution costs

A business organisation performs a number of functions, e.g., production, illustration, selling and distribution, research and development. Costs are to be curtained for each of these functions. The Chartered Institute of Management accountants, London, has defined each of the above costs as follows:

Production cost

The cost of sequence of operations which begins with supplying materials, labour and services and ends with the primary packing of the product. Thus, it includes the cost of direct material, direct labour, direct expenses and factory overheads.

Administration cost

The cost of formulating the policy, directing the organisation and controlling the operations of an undertaking which is not related directly to a production, selling, distribution, research or development activity or function.

Selling cost

It is the cost of selling to create and stimulate demand (sometimes termed as marketing) and of securing orders.

Distribution cost

It is the cost of sequence of operations beginning with making the packed product available for dispatch and ending with making the reconditioned returned empty package, if any, available for reuse.

Research cost

It is the cost of searching for new or improved products, new application of materials, or new or improved methods.

Development cost

The cost of process which begins with the implementation of the decision to produce a new or improved product or employ a new or improved method and ends with the commencement of formal production of that product or by the method.

Pre-Production cost

The part of development cost incurred in making a trial production as preliminary to formal production is called pre-production cost.

15. Conversion cost

The cost of transforming direct materials into finished products excluding direct material cost is known as conversion cost. It is usually taken as an aggregate of total cost of direct labour, direct expenses and factory overheads.

Cost unit and cost center

The technique of costing involves the following:

— Collection and classification of expenditure according to cost elements

— Allocation and apportionment of the expenditure to the cost centers or cost units or both

Cost Unit

While preparing cost accounts, it becomes necessary to select a unit with which expenditure may be identified. The quantity upon which cost can be conveniently allocated is known as a unit of cost or cost unit. The Chartered Institute of Management Accountants, London defines a unit of cost as a unit of quantity of product, service or time in relation to which costs may be ascertained or expressed.

Cost center

Cost center refers to one of the convenient units into which the whole factory or an organisation has been appropriately divided for costing purposes. Each such unit consists of a department, a sub-department or an item or equipment or machinery and a person or a group of persons. Sometimes, closely associated departments are combined together and considered as one unit for costing purposes. For example, in a laundry, activities such as collecting, sorting, marking and washing of clothes are performed. Each activity may be considered as a separate cost center and all costs relating to a particular cost center may be found out separately.

Cost centers may be classified as follows:

— Productive, unproductive and mixed cost centers

— Personal and impersonal cost centers

— Operation and process cost centers

Productive cost centers are those which are actually engaged in making products. Service or unproductive cost centers do not make the products but act as the essential aids for the productive centers. The examples of such service centers are as follows:

— Administration department

— Repairs and maintenance department

— Stores and drawing office department

Mixed costs centers are those which are engaged sometimes on productive and other times on service works. For example, a tool shop serves as a productive cost center when it manufactures dies and jigs to be charged to specific jobs or orders but serves as servicing cost center when it does repairs for the factory.

Impersonal cost center is one which consists of a department, a plant or an item of equipment whereas a personal cost center consists of a person or a group of persons. In case a cost center consists of those machines or persons which carry out the same operation, it is termed as operation cost center. If a cost center consists of a continuous sequence of operations, it is called process cost center.

In case of an operation cost center, cost is analysed and related to a series of operations in sequence such as in chemical industries, oil refineries and other process industries. The objective of such an analysis is to ascertain the cost of each operation irrespective of its location inside the factory.

Objectives of Cost Accounting

The main objectives of cost accounting as follows:

— *Determining selling price :* Business enterprises run on a profit-making basis. It is, thus, necessary that revenue should be greater than expenditure incurred in producing goods and services from which the revenue is to be derived. Cost accounting provides various information regarding the cost to make and sell such products or services. Of course, many other factors such as the condition of market, the area of distribution, the quantity which can be supplied etc. are also given due consideration by management before deciding upon the price but the cost plays a dominating role.

— *Determining and controlling efficiency :* Cost accounting involves a study of various operations used in manufacturing a product or providing a service. The study facilitates measuring the efficiency of an organisation as a whole or department-wise as well as devising means of increasing efficiency.

Cost accounting also uses a number of methods, e.g., budgetary control, standard costing etc. for controlling costs. Each item viz. materials, labour and expenses is budgeted at the commencement of a period and actual expenses incurred are compared with budget. This greatly increases the operating efficiency of an enterprise.

— *Facilitating preparation of financial and other statements :* The third objective of cost accounting is to produce statements whenever is required by management. The financial statements are prepared under financial accounting generally once a year or half-year and are spaced too far with respect to time to meet the needs of management. In order to operate a business at a high level of efficiency, it is essential for management to have a frequent review of production, sales and operating results. Cost accounting provides daily, weekly or monthly volumes of units produced and accumulated costs with appropriate analysis. A developed cost accounting system provides immediate information regarding stock of raw materials, work-in-progress and finished goods. This helps in speedy preparation of financial statements.

Basis for Operating Policy

Cost accounting helps management to formulate operating policies. These policies may relate to any of the following matters:

— Determination of a cost-volume-profit relationship

— Shutting down or operating at a loss

— Making for or buying from outside suppliers

— Continuing with the existing plant and machinery or replacing them by improved and economic ones

Cost Estimation and Ascertainment

Cost estimation is the process of pre-determining the cost of a certain product job or order. Such pre-determination may be required for several purposes. Some of the purposes are as follows:

— Budgeting

— Measurement of performance efficiency

— Preparation of financial statements (valuation of stocks etc.)

— Make or buy decisions

— Fixation of the sale prices of products

Cost ascertainment is the process of determining costs on the basis of actual data. Hence, the computation of historical cost is cost ascertainment while the computation of future costs is cost estimation. Both cost estimation and cost ascertainment are interrelated and are of immense use to the management. In case a concern has a sound costing system, the ascertained costs will greatly help the management in the process of estimation of rational accurate costs which are necessary for a variety of purposes stated above. Moreover, the ascertained cost may be compared with the pre-determined costs on a continuing basis and proper and timely steps be taken for controlling costs and maximising profits.

Cost Allocation and Apportionment

Cost allocation and cost apportionment are the two procedures which describe the identification and allotment of costs to cost centers or cost units. Cost allocation refers to the allotment of all the items of cost to cost centers or cost units whereas cost apportionment refers to the allotment of proportions of items of cost to cost centers or cost units Thus, the former involves the process of charging direct expenditure to cost centers or cost units whereas the latter involves the process of charging indirect expenditure to cost centers or cost units.

For example, the cost of labour engaged in a service department can be charged wholly and directly but the canteen expenses of the factory cannot be charged directly and wholly. Its proportionate share will have to be found out. Charging of costs in the former case will be termed as "allocation of costs" whereas in the latter, it will be termed as "apportionment of costs."

Cost Reduction and Control

Cost reduction and cost control are two different concepts. Cost control is achieving the cost target as its objective whereas cost reduction is directed to explore the possibilities of improving the targets. Thus, cost control ends when targets are achieved whereas cost reduction has no visible end. It is a continuous process. The difference between the two can be summarised as follows:

Cost control aims at maintaining the costs in accordance with established standards whereas cost reduction is concerned with reducing costs. It changes all standards and endeavors to improve them continuously.

Cost control seeks to attain the lowest possible cost under existing conditions whereas cost reduction does not recognise any condition as permanent since a change will result in lowering the cost. In case of cost control, emphasis is on past and present. In case of cost reduction, emphasis is on the present and future.

Cost control is a preventive function whereas cost reduction is a correlative function. It operates even when an efficient cost control system exists.

Installation of Costing System

The installation of a costing system requires careful consideration of the following two interrelated aspects:

— Overcoming the practical difficulties while introducing a system

— Main considerations that should govern the installation of such a system

Practical Difficulties

The important difficulties in the installation of a costing system and the suggestions to overcome them are as follows:

a. Lack of support from top management

Often, the costing system is introduced at the behest of the managing director or some other director without taking into confidence other members of the top management team. This results in opposition from various managers as they consider it interference as well as an uncalled check of their activities. They, therefore, resist the additional work involved in the cost accounting system.

This difficulty can be overcome by taking the top management into confidence before installing the system. A sense of cost consciousness has to be instilled in their minds.

b. Resistance from the staff

The existing financial accounting staff may offer resistance to the system because of a feeling of their being declared redundant under the new system. This fear can be overcome by explaining the staff that the costing system would not replace but strengthen the existing system. It will open new areas for development which will prove beneficial to them.

c. Non-cooperation at other levels

The foreman and other supervisory staff may resent the additional paper work and may not cooperate in providing the basic data which is essential for the success of the system. This needs re-orientation and education of employees. They have to be told of the advantages that will accrue to them and to the organisation as a whole on account of efficient working of the system.

d. Shortage of trained staff

Costing is a specialised job in itself. In the beginning, a qualified staff may not be available. However, this difficulty can be overcome by giving the existing staff requisite training and recruiting additional staff if required.

e. Heavy costs

The costing system will involve heavy costs unless it has been suitably designed to meet specific requirements. Unnecessary sophistication and formalities should be avoided. The costing office should serve as a useful service department.

Main Considerations

The following should be the main considerations while introducing a costing system in a manufacturing organisation:

1. Product

The nature of a product determines to a great extent the type of costing system to be adopted. A product requiring high value of material content requires an elaborate system of materials control. Similarly, a product requiring high value of labour content requires an efficient time keeping and wage systems. The same is true in case of overheads.

2. *Organisation*

The existing organisation structure should be distributed as little as possible. It becomes, therefore, necessary to ascertain the size and type of organisation before introducing the costing system. The scope of authority of each executive, the sources from which a cost accountant has to derive information and reports to be submitted at various managerial levels should be carefully gone through.

3. *Objective*

The objectives and information which management wants to achieve and acquire should also be taken care of. For example, if a concern wants to expand its operations, the system of costing should be designed in a way so as to give maximum attention to production aspect. On the other hand, if a concern were not in a position to sell its products, the selling aspect would require greater attention.

4. *Technical details*

The system should be introduced after a detailed study of the technical aspects of the business. Efforts should be made to secure the sympathetic assistance and support of the principal members of the supervisory staff and workmen.

5. *Informative and simple*

The system should be informative and simple. In this connection, the following points may be noted:

(i) It should be capable of furnishing the fullest information required regularly and systematically, so that continuous study or check-up of the progress of business is possible.

(ii) Standard printed forms can be used so as to make the information detailed, clear and intelligible. Over-elaboration which will only complicate matters should be avoided.

(iii) Full information about departmental outputs, processes and operations should be clearly presented and every item of expenditure should be properly classified.

(iv) Data, complete and reliable in all respects should be provided in a lucid form so that the measurement of the variations between actual and standard costs is possible.

6. Method of Maintenance of Cost Records

A choice has to be made between integral and non-integral accounting systems. In case of integral accounting system, no separate sets of books are maintained for costing transactions but they are interlocked with financial transactions into one set of books. In case of non-integral system, separate books are maintained for cost and financial transactions. At the end of the accounting period, the results shown by two sets of books are reconciled. In case of a big business, it will be appropriate to maintain a separate set of books for cost transactions.

7. Elasticity

The costing system should be elastic and capable of adapting to the changing requirements of a business. It may, therefore, be concluded from the above discussion that costing system introduced in any business will not be a success in case of the following circumstances:

— If it is unduly complicated and expensive
— If a cost accountant does not get the cooperation of his/her staff
— If cost statements cannot be reconciled with financial statements
— If the results actually achieved are not compared with the expected ones

Methods of Costing

Costing can be defined as the technique and process of ascertaining costs. The principles in every method of costing are same but the methods of analysing and presenting the costs differ with the nature of business. The methods of job costing are as follows:

1. *Job costing*

The system of job costing is used where production is not highly repetitive and in addition consists of distinct jobs so that the material and labour costs can be identified by order number. This method of costing is very common in commercial foundries and drop forging shops and in plants making specialised industrial equipments. In all these cases, an account is opened for each job and all appropriate expenditure is charged thereto.

2. *Contract costing*

Contract costing does not in principle differ from job costing. A contract is a big job whereas a job is a small contract. The term is usually applied where large-scale contracts are carried out. In case of ship-builders, printers, building contractors etc., this system of costing is used. Job or contract is also termed as terminal costing.

3. Cost plus costing

In contracts where in addition to cost, an agreed sum or percentage to cover overheads and fit is paid to a contractor, the system is termed as cost plus costing. The term cost here includes materials, labour and expenses incurred directly in the process of production. The system is used generally in cases where government happens to be the party to give contract.

4. Batch costing

This method is employed where orders or jobs are arranged in different batches after taking into account the convenience of producing articles. The unit of cost is a batch or a group of identical products instead of a single job order or contract. This method is particularly suitable for general engineering factories which produce components in convenient economic batches and pharmaceutical industries.

5. Process costing

If a product passes through different stages, each distinct and well defined, it is desired to know the cost of production at each stage. In order to ascertain the same, process costing is employed under which a separate account is opened for each process. This system of costing is suitable for the extractive industries, e.g., chemical manufacture, paints, foods, explosives, soap making etc.

6. Operation costing

Operation costing is a further refinement of process costing. The system is employed in the industries of the following types:

— The industry in which mass or repetitive production is carried out

— The industry in which articles or components have to be stocked in semi-finished stage to facilitate the execution of special orders, or for the convenience of issue for later operations

The procedure of costing is broadly the same as process costing except that in this case, cost unit is an operation instead of a process. For example, the manufacturing of handles for bicycles involves a number of operations such as those of cutting steel sheets into proper strips molding, machining and finally polishing. The cost to complete these operations may be found out separately.

7. Unit costing (Output Costing or Single Costing)

In this method, cost per unit of output or production is ascertained and the amount of each element constituting such cost is determined. In case where the products can be expressed in identical quantitative units and where manufacture is continuous, this type of costing is applied. Cost statements or cost sheets are prepared in which various items of expense are classified and the total expenditure is divided by the total quantity produced in order to arrive at per unit cost of production. The method is suitable in industries like brick making, collieries, flour mills, paper mills, cement manufacturing etc.

8. Operating Costing

This system is employed where expenses are incurred for provision of services such as those tendered by bus companies, electricity companies, or railway companies. The total expenses regarding operation are divided by the appropriate units (e.g., in case of bus company, total number of passenger/kms.) and cost per unit of service is calculated.

9. Departmental Costing

The ascertainment of the cost of output of each department separately is the objective of departmental costing. In case where a factory is divided into a number of departments, this method is adopted.

10. Multiple Costing (Composite Costing)

Under this system, the costs of different sections of production are combined after finding out the cost of each and every part manufactured. The system of ascertaining cost in this way is applicable where a product comprises many assailable parts, e.g., motor cars, engines or machine tools, typewrite$, radios, cycles etc.

As various components differ from each other in a variety of ways such as price, materials used and manufacturing processes, a separate method of costing is employed in respect of each component. The type of costing where more than one method of costing is employed is called multiple costing.

It is to be noted that basically there are only two methods of costing viz. job costing and process costing. Job costing is employed in cases where expenses are traceable to specific jobs or orders, e.g., house building, ship building etc. In case where it is impossible to trace the prime cost of the items for a particular order because of the reason that their identity gets lost while manufacturing operations, process costing is used. For example, in a refinery where several tons of oil is being produced at the same time, the prime cost of a specific order of 10 tons cannot be traced. The cost can be found out only by finding out the cost per ton of total oil produced and then multiplying it by ten.

It may, therefore, be concluded that the methods of batch contract and cost plus costing are only the variants of job costing whereas the methods of unit, operation and operating costing are the variants of process costing.

Techniques of Costing

Besides the above methods of costing, following are the types of costing techniques which are used by management only for controlling costs and making some important managerial decisions. As a matter of fact, they are not independent methods of cost finding such as job or process costing but are basically costing techniques which can be used as an advantage with any of the methods discussed above.

1. *Marginal costing*

Marginal costing is a technique of costing in which allocation of expenditure to production is restricted to those expenses which arise as a result of production, e.g., materials, labour, direct expenses and variable overheads. Fixed overheads are excluded in cases where production varies because it may give misleading results. The technique is useful in manufacturing industries with varying levels of output.

2. *Direct costing*

The practice of charging all direct costs to operations, processes or products and leaving all indirect costs to be written off against profits in the period in which they arise is termed as direct costing. The technique differs from marginal costing because some fixed costs can be considered as direct costs in appropriate circumstances.

3. *Absorption or full costing*

The practice of charging all costs both variable and fixed

to operations, products or processes is termed as absorption costing.

4. Uniform costing

A technique where standardised principles and methods of cost accounting are employed by a number of different companies and firms is termed as uniform costing. Standardisation may extend to the methods of costing, accounting classification including codes, methods of defining costs and charging depreciation, methods of allocating or apportioning overheads to cost centers or cost units. The system, thus, facilitates inter- firm comparisons, establishment of realistic pricing policies, etc.

Systems of Costing

It has already been stated that there are two main methods used to determine costs. These are:

— Job cost method

— Process cost method

It is possible to ascertain the costs under each of the above methods by two different ways:

— Historical costing

— Standard costing

Historical costing

Historical costing can be of the following two types in nature:

— Post costing

— Continuous costing

Post costing

Post costing means ascertainment of cost after the

production is completed. This is done by analysing the financial accounts at the end of a period in such a way so as to disclose the cost of the units which have been produced.

For instance, if the cost of product A is to be calculated on this basis, one will have to wait till the materials are actually purchased and used, labour actually paid and overhead expenditure actually incurred. This system is used only for ascertaining the costs but not useful for exercising any control over costs, as one comes to know of things after they had taken place. It can serve as guidance for future production only when conditions in future continue to be the same.

Continuous costing

In case of this method, cost is ascertained as soon as a job is completed or even when a job is in progress. This is done usually before a job is over or product is made. In the process, actual expenditure on materials and wages and share of overheads are also estimated. Hence, the figure of cost ascertained in this case is not exact. But it has an advantage of providing cost information to the management promptly, thereby enabling it to take necessary corrective action on time. However, it neither provides any standard for judging current efficiency nor does it disclose what the cost of a job ought to have been.

Standard costing

Standard costing is a system under which the cost of a product is determined in advance on certain pre-determined standards. With reference to the example given in post costing, the cost of product A can be calculated in advance if one is in a position to estimate in advance the material labour and overheads that should be incurred over the product. All this requires an efficient system of cost accounting. However, this system will not be useful if a vigorous system of controlling costs and standard costs are not in force. Standard costing is becoming more and more popular nowadays.

Marginal Costing and Absorption Costing

Marginal costing distinguishes between fixed costs and variable costs as convention ally classified. Marginal costing is formally defined as: 'the accounting system in which variable costs are charged to cost units and the fixed costs of the period are written-off in full against the aggregate contribution. Its special value is in decision making'.

The term 'contribution' mentioned in the formal definition is the term given to the difference between Sales and Marginal cost. Thus

Marginal cost = Variable cost Direct Labour +

Direct Material + Direct Expense + Variable Overheads

Contribution sales - Marginal Cost

The term marginal cost sometimes refers to the marginal cost per unit and sometimes to the total marginal costs of a department or batch or operation. The meaning is usually clear from the context.

Theory of Marginal Costing

The theory of marginal costing may, therefore, by understood in the following two steps:

— If the volume of output increases, the cost per unit in normal circumstances reduces. Conversely, if an output reduces, the cost per unit increases. If a factory produces 1000 units at a total cost of $3,000 and if by increasing the output by one unit the cost goes up to

$3,002, the marginal cost of additional output will be $.2.

— If an increase in output is more than one, the total increase in cost divided by the total increase in output will give the average marginal cost per unit. If, for example, the output is increased to 1020 units from 1000 units and the total cost to produce these units is $1,045, the average marginal cost per unit is $2.25. It can be described as follows:

Additional cost = Additional units $ 45 = $2.25 20

The ascertainment of marginal cost is based on the classification and segregation of cost into fixed and variable cost. In order to understand the marginal costing technique, it is essential to understand the meaning of marginal cost.

Marginal cost means the cost of the marginal or last unit produced. It is also defined as the cost of one more or one less unit produced besides existing level of production. In this connection, a unit may mean a single commodity, a dozen, a gross or any other measure of goods.

For example, if a manufacturing firm produces X unit at a cost of $ 300 and X+1 units at a cost of $ 320, the cost of an additional unit will be $ 20 which is marginal cost. Similarly if the production of X-1 units comes down to $ 280, the cost of marginal unit will be $ 20 (300–280).

The marginal cost varies directly with the volume of production and marginal cost per unit remains the same. It consists of prime cost, i.e. cost of direct materials, direct labour and all variable overheads. It does not contain any element of fixed cost which is kept separate under marginal cost technique.

Marginal costing may be defined as the technique of presenting cost data wherein variable costs and fixed costs are shown separately for managerial decision-making. It should be clearly understood that marginal costing is not a method of costing like process costing or job costing.

There are different phrases being used for this technique of costing. In UK, marginal costing is a popular phrase whereas in US, it is known as direct costing and is used in place of marginal costing. Variable costing is another name of marginal costing. Marginal costing technique has given birth to a very useful concept of contribution where contribution is given by: Sales revenue less variable cost (marginal cost)

Contribution may be defined as the profit before the recovery of fixed costs. Thus, contribution goes toward the recovery of fixed cost and profit, and is equal to fixed cost plus profit (C = F + P). In case a firm neither makes profit nor suffers loss, contribution will be just equal to fixed cost (C = F). this is known as break even point. The concept of contribution is very useful in marginal costing. It has a fixed relation with sales. The proportion of contribution to sales is known as P/V ratio which remains the same under given conditions of production and sales.

Principles of Marginal Costing

The principles of marginal costing are as follows. For any given period of time, fixed costs will be the same, for any volume of sales and production (provided that the level of activity is within the 'relevant range'). Therefore, by selling an extra item of product or service the following will happen.

— Revenue will increase by the sales value of the item sold.

— Costs will increase by the variable cost per unit.
— Profit will increase by the amount of contribution earned from the extra item.

Profit measurement should therefore be based on an analysis of total contribution. Since fixed costs relate to a period of time, and do not change with increases or decreases in sales volume, it is misleading to charge units of sale with a share of fixed costs. When a unit of product is made, the extra costs incurred in its manufacture are the variable production costs. Fixed costs are unaffected, and no extra fixed costs are incurred when output is increased.

Features of Marginal Costing

The main features of marginal costing are as follows:

Cost classification

The marginal costing technique makes a sharp distinction between variable costs and fixed costs. It is the variable cost on the basis of which production and sales policies are designed by a firm following the marginal costing technique.

Stock/Inventory Valuation

Under marginal costing, inventory/stock for profit measurement is valued at marginal cost. It is in sharp contrast to the total unit cost under absorption costing method.

Marginal contribution

Marginal costing technique makes use of marginal contribution for marking various decisions. Marginal contribution is the difference between sales and marginal cost. It forms the basis for judging the profitability of different products or departments.

Advantages of marginal costing technique

— Marginal costing is simple to understand.

— By not charging fixed overhead to cost of production, the effect of varying charges per unit is avoided.

— It prevents the illogical carry forward in stock valuation of some proportion of current year's fixed overhead.

— The effects of alternative sales or production policies can be more readily available and assessed, and decisions taken would yield the maximum return to business.

— It eliminates large balances left in overhead control accounts which indicate the difficulty of ascertaining an accurate overhead recovery rate.

— Practical cost control is greatly facilitated. By avoiding arbitrary allocation of fixed overhead, efforts can be concentrated on maintaining a uniform and consistent marginal cost. It is useful to various levels of management.

— It helps in short-term profit planning by breakeven and profitability analysis, both in terms of quantity and graphs. Comparative profitability and performance between two or more products and divisions can easily be assessed and brought to the notice of management for decision making.

Disadvantages of marginal costing technique

— The separation of costs into fixed and variable is difficult and sometimes gives misleading results.

— Normal costing systems also apply overhead under normal operating volume and this shows that no advantage is gained by marginal costing.

— Under marginal costing, stocks and work in progress are understated. The exclusion of fixed costs from inventories affect profit, and true and fair view of financial affairs of an organisation may not be clearly transparent.

— Volume variance in standard costing also discloses the effect of fluctuating output on fixed overhead. Marginal cost data becomes unrealistic in case of highly fluctuating levels of production, e.g., in case of seasonal factories.

— Application of fixed overhead depends on estimates and not on the actuals and as such there may be under or over absorption of the same.

— Control affected by means of budgetary control is also accepted by many. In order to know the net profit, we should not be satisfied with contribution and hence, fixed overhead is also a valuable item. A system which ignores fixed costs is less effective since a major portion of fixed cost is not taken care of under marginal costing.

— In practice, sales price, fixed cost and variable cost per unit may vary. Thus, the assumptions underlying the theory of marginal costing sometimes becomes unrealistic. For long term profit planning, absorption costing is the only answer.

Presentation of Cost Data

Marginal costing is not a method of costing but a technique of presentation of sales and cost data with a view to guide management in decision-making. The traditional technique popularly known as total cost or absorption costing technique does not make any difference between variable and fixed cost in the calculation of profits. But marginal cost statement very clearly indicates this difference in arriving at the net operational results of a firm.

Marginal Costing versus Absorption Costing

After knowing the two techniques of marginal costing and absorption costing, we have seen that the net profits are not the same because of the following reasons:

1. Over and under absorbed overheads

In absorption costing, fixed overheads can never be absorbed exactly because of difficulty in forecasting costs and volume of output. If these balances of under or over absorbed/recovery are not written off to costing profit and loss account, the actual amount incurred is not shown in it. In marginal costing, however, the actual fixed overhead incurred is wholly charged against contribution and hence, there will be some difference in net profits.

2. Difference in stock valuation

In marginal costing, work in progress and finished stocks are valued at marginal cost, but in absorption costing, they are valued at total production cost. Hence, profit will differ as different amounts of fixed overheads are considered in two accounts.

The profit difference due to difference in stock valuation is summarised as follows:

- When there is no opening and closing stocks, there will be no difference in profit.
- When opening and closing stocks are same, there will be no difference in profit, provided the fixed cost

element in opening and closing stocks are of the same amount.

— When closing stock is more than opening stock, the profit under absorption costing will be higher as comparatively a greater portion of fixed cost is included in closing stock and carried over to next period.

— When closing stock is less than opening stock, the profit under absorption costing will be less as comparatively a higher amount of fixed cost contained in opening stock is debited during the current period.

The features which distinguish marginal costing from absorption costing are as follows:

— In absorption costing, items of stock are costed to include a 'fair share' of fixed production overhead, whereas in marginal costing, stocks are valued at variable production cost only. The value of closing stock will be higher in absorption costing than in marginal costing.

— As a consequence of carrying forward an element of fixed production overheads in closing stock values, the cost of sales used to determine profit in absorption costing will:

  — include some fixed production overhead costs incurred in a previous period but carried forward into opening stock values of the current period;

  — exclude some fixed production overhead costs incurred in the current period by including them in closing stock values.

— In contrast marginal costing charges the actual fixed costs of a period in full into the profit and loss account of the period. (Marginal costing is therefore sometimes known as period costing.)

- In absorption costing, 'actual' fully absorbed unit costs are reduced by producing in greater quantities, whereas in marginal costing, unit variable costs are unaffected by the volume of production (that is, provided that variable costs per unit remain unaltered at the changed level of production activity). Profit per unit in any period can be affected by the actual volume of production in absorption costing; this is not the case in marginal costing.
- In marginal costing, the identification of variable costs and of contribution enables management to use cost information more easily for decision-making purposes (such as in budget decision making). It is easy to decide by how much contribution (and therefore profit) will be affected by changes in sales volume. (Profit would be unaffected by changes in production volume).
- In absorption costing, however, the effect on profit in a period of changes in both:
  - production volume; and
  - sales volume;
  - is not easily seen, because behaviour is not analysed and incremental costs are not used in the calculation of actual profit.

Limitations of Absorption Costing

The following are the criticisms against absorption costing:

- You might have observed that in absorption costing, a portion of fixed cost is carried over to the subsequent accounting period as part of closing stock. This is an unsound practice because costs pertaining to a period should not be allowed to be vitiated by the inclusion of costs pertaining to the previous period and vice versa.

— Further, absorption costing is dependent on the levels of output which may vary from period to period, and consequently cost per unit changes due to the existence of fixed overhead. Unless fixed overhead rate is based on normal capacity, such changed costs are not helpful for the purposes of comparison and control.

The cost to produce an extra unit is variable production cost. It is realistic to the value of closing stock items as this is a directly attributable cost. The size of total contribution varies directly with sales volume at a constant rate per unit. For the decision-making purpose of management, better information about expected profit is obtained from the use of variable costs and contribution approach in the accounting system.

3

Budgeting and Budgetary Controls

In non-commercial food and beverage operations, budgets are just as important. They help to ensure that planned expenses do not exceed anticipated revenues and, if required, that an operating surplus ("profit") can be generated. An operating budget is not an obstacle to efficient performance to be prepared and followed only when top management insists. In fact, operating budgets are critical for planning the profit requirements of food and beverage operations.

The budget is your best forecast for the future. Operating budgets are an excellent source of estimated revenue and cost information, which can represent planned performance standards. Actual operating data can be compared against budgeted information to determine the extent to which financial plans are attained.

Control Process

An operating budget is a plan that estimates how much revenue will be generated and what expenses will be incurred to meet financial requirements and goals. There are several different types of budgets-for example: long- and shortterm, capital and cash. The type of budget most useful to a food and beverage operation is a shortterm, (one-year) operating budget, which covers items affecting the income statement. The budget is a constant reminder of the amount of revenue planed. And, just as crucial for purposes of control, information stemming from the budget limits the amount of allowable expenses. If these limits are exceeded, budgeted profits decrease unless expenses are reduced in other areas and/ or revenue increases beyond the anticipated level.

Once developed, the budget becomes an important part of the control process. The budget plan tells managers how much money can be spent in each expense category. When actual revenue falls below forecasted levels and/ or when actual expenses exceed budget estimates, managers know there may be problems. Corrective action can then be implemented on a timely basis. A current period's budget is used to develop the budgets for the next fiscal period. Information from the current budget is the basis for beginning the budget process for the next fiscal year.

Because the budget provides anticipated revenue and cost figures, it enables the calculation of a budgeted food cost percentage (budgeted food cost divided by budgeted food revenue multiplied by 100) and a budgeted beverage cost percentage (budgeted beverage cost divided by budgeted beverage revenue multiplied by 100). In a similar way, benchmarks for all other expenses-such as labour and energy costs-can also be calculated. These budget percentages can later be compared with percentages representing actual operating results to measure the food and beverage manager's effectiveness in meeting budget goals.

Managers have two special concerns when they establish operating budget standards. The goals set for revenue, profit requirements, and operating expenses must be attainable and must not compromise established quality requirements. H standards are impossible to attain, personnel may get frustrated and the operation could deteriorate. For example, if food costs have averaged 45 percent, achieving a budgeted goal of 38 percent may not be possible, at least within a single fiscal period. Furthermore, food and beverage managers are concerned about quality standards.

Management should set minimum quality standards based upon the expectations of the target markets. This helps ensure that standards will not be compromised as the budget plan is developed and implemented. When necessary, management can use the budget not only to evaluate past efforts but also to plan corrective action for the future. Since the budget helps define responsibilities, management personnel can be held responsible for meeting revenue goals and keeping all operating costs within budgeted limits.

When budget figures are exceeded or underspent, responsibility can correctly be assigned to the manager in charge. In small food and beverage operations, the owner/manager generally develops the budget. In larger operations, other staff members provide important help. For example, department heads, whose performance will be judged by the extent to which they attain budget goals, might be assigned to plan expense levels for their areas of responsibility, in consultation with senior management personnel. In still larger operations, a budget committee may review department revenue and expense plans before a final property-wide budget is approved.

Budgeting in Multi-Unit Operations

There are basically two methods used to develop operating budgets in multiunit operations. The most common method uses a bottom-up budgeting approach m which operating budgets are assembled at the unit level and are "rolled" up the organisation. Another approach is referred to as top-down budgeting. With this plans budgets are developed at the corporate level and are then passed down to lower organisational levels with each successively lower level becoming responsible for a specific segment of the budget.

The main advantage of using bottom-up budgeting is that budget plans are specifically geared to the individual operation. When budgets are developed for a specific operation by the unit manager, the lower level participation yields a budget that is "our plan," not a plan thrust upon lower management by higher organisational levels. The "ownership" this creates helps the unit manager recognise the importance-and feasibility-of the operating budget. Likewise, bottom-up budgeting enables budget planners to focus on specific units and special problems that are likely to be encountered.

Unfortunately, corporate-level managers encounter a problem when the sum of profits anticipated by individual units generating their own operating budgets, does not equal the profit requirements of the corporation. For example a restaurant company may be owned by a parent organisation that mandates a profit contribution larger than that which is planned to be generated by the individual units. This points to an advantage of top-down budgeting.

In addition to helping plan for corporate-level profit expectations top-down budgeting has other potential advantages. For example, unit managers in specific properties may not be aware of marketing commitments advertising campaigns menu charges and other factors that can have a significant impact upon operating budgets within an individual unit.

In actual practice budget planners in multiunit organisations use a give-and take method that first develops tentative budget plans and then modifies them to be realistic expectations for individual properties. Psychological aspects of budget development must also be considered and incorporated into budget development strategies. For example unit managers may wish to send conservative estimates "up the organisation," and conversely, top-level managers may wish to suggest more aggressive budget goals.

Budget Reforecasting

Budgets are developed several months before the start of the food and beverage operation's fiscal year. As such future events that affect revenue and expense levels cannot be accurately forecasted. Since the operating budget is a critical control tool it is important to have updated information against which to compare actual operating results.

Many food and beverage operations use a method of reforecasting to update budgets. For example if revenue trends are significantly different than expected revised revenue estimates for the budget may be developed. This same approach is used to consider realistic expense estimates based upon actual performance during the earlier parts of the budget year. Reforecasting is most easily accomplished when all expenses are expressed as a percentage of revenue. Then, as revenue estimates increase or decrease, affected operating expenses can be adjusted accordingly.

When reforecasting is done, food and beverage managers can use information from income statements to compare actual operating results with:

— Budgeted revenue and expense levels-both for the current period and for cumulative to-date results during the operating year.

— Reforecasted revenue and expense information-both for the month and fiscal year-to-date.

Steps of Budget Development

There are three major steps in the process of developing a budget. First, forecasts of expected revenue are determined. Second, required profit levels for the food and beverage operation are calculated. Third, an appropriate method is used to calculate projected costs incurred in generating the forecasted revenue. Although it is useful to divide the process of budget development into these three steps, the last two steps really belong to the same phase of budget development because the profit requirement can be regarded as one of the" costs" assessed in calculating expenses.

Step 1: Calculate Projected Revenue Levels

The first step in the budget development process is to estimate revenue levels. fu hotel and restaurant operations, forecasts are normally made separately for food and beverage revenues. This helps managers pinpoint operating problems during the budget period. When budgets are based on combined food and beverage revenues, managers may not be able to easily identify operating problems during the budget period. However, when accurate guest check averages are available, some managers combine food and beverage revenues when developing budgets. In this case, revenue forecasts are based on the number of guests anticipated for the period covered by the budget. Revenue forecasts are determined by multiplying the number of anticipated guests by the amount of the average guest check. Depending on a number of other factors, this forecast may be increased (for example, if selling prices are planned to increase during the period covered by the budget) or decreased.

Projected revenue calculations should be made at least monthly. Calculating revenue projections on a weekly basis would provide even more specific information and perhaps increased accuracy. Individual estimates can then be combined into an annual revenue forecast. By using either monthly or weekly projections, actual revenue can later be compared with budgeted revenue-and actual expenses with budgeted expenses-in time for corrective action, if necessary. Generally figures for past revenue levels can be obtained from monthly income statements. Collecting revenue figures is made relatively easy by today's common use of computerised systems that list monthly cumulative "todate" statistics. This also makes it easy to notice trends between fiscal periods.

There are many factors that affect the development of revenue forecasts. In fact anything that can influence revenue levels also affects the development of revenue forecasts. For instance, internal sales promotion plans or scheduled remodeling could have a strong impact on revenue. Consequently, projected revenue for the coming fiscal period may need to be adjusted to account for these plans. Important factors to consider in determining revenue estimates include revenue histories, current factors, economic variables, and other factors.

Revenue histories: Useful forecasts for the new budget period can be developed by analysing past revenue levels and identifying trends. For example, if examining revenue histories shows that food and beverage revenue has increased by an average of eight percent for each of the past five years, then revenue for the upcoming period could be estimated by simply adding eight percent to the current revenue level. This assumes that the revenue growth of the past will continue in the future.

Current factors: There are many factors over which the property has little or no control that may affect revenue during the new budget period. For example, new competition, street improvement projects, or even the weather may have a strong impact on revenue levels. Social issues, such as liability laws regarding the sale and service of alcoholic beverages, may affect alcoholic beverage revenue. Budgeted revenue figures that are based on revenue histories and trend studies would need to be adjusted if any of these factors currently affect the property.

Economic variables: As costs increase during periods of high inflation, selling prices for food and beverage products must also be increased. At the same time, the public's habits and lifestyles are affected by economic conditions. When inflation rises, guests may demand greater value for their money. Some guests may "trade down" and replace their usual dining experiences with less expensive meals in lower-priced restaurants. Other guests may simply "trade out" and enjoy more meals at home with their families.

Other factors: Properties offering both food and beverages must estimate total revenue levels for both services. As noted previously, when making projections for food and beverage operations, revenue and expenses should normally be kept separate so that, subsequently, each can be controlled separately. Many lodging properties use the concept of derived demand, in which estimates of room revenue are used to help project revenue from food, beverages, and other revenue centers based upon guest spending patterns that have been developed from in-house studies. The hotel food and beverage manager must still calculate the impact of banquet operations and local community spending patterns separately to determine the total operating budget for the food and beverage department.

Forecasting beverage revenue: Few small beverage operations develop specific budget revenue estimates for individual beverage products such as beer, wine, liquor, and soft drinks. Rather, they assume that each beverage product will generate the same percentage of total beverage revenue in each budget period. For example, if liquor has been responsible for 70 percent of beverage revenue in past years, beverage managers may assume that it will continue to contribute 70 percent of future beverage revenue. However, beverage managers should carefully review trends in these percentage-of-revenue statistics. Wine sparkling water, and nonalcoholic specialty drinks are generating an increased proportion of beverage revenue in many places. Where this is true, other products, such as liquor, will contribute a reduced percentage of revenue.

Decisions regarding the percentage of total beverage revenue applicable to each product are relatively easy to make when electronic cash registers or other point-of sale devices are used to record information about beverage revenue by category. In operations that do not use computerised equipment or keep records on this basis, it may be necessary to base product revenue percentages on administrative judgment. In this case, perhaps a trial period for keeping careful product revenue records may provide some hard data to back up estimates of product revenue percentages.

Step 2: Determine Profit Requirements

There are two basic ways to treat profit when budgets are developed: (1) regarding profit as "what is left over from revenue after subtracting expenses," and (2) treating profit as if it were a "cost." The traditional approach determines profit by deducting estimated expenses from forecasted revenue:

$$\text{Profit} = \text{Revenue} - \text{Expenses}$$

A better approach treats profit as a "cost." This approach determines profit requirements before estimating expenses so that, in effect, the property pays itself first. Money remaining after profit requirements have been deducted from revenue is then used to pay for the operation's expenses. While the traditional method uses estimated expense levels to determine profit, this approach uses forecasted revenue and required profit levels to determine allowable expenses:

Revenue - Required Profit = Allowable Operating Expenses

With this formula, the food and beverage manager is concerned about achieving budgeted profit levels while at the same time assuring sufficient revenue to meet expenses. Using this plan for developing a budget, the food and beverage manager wants to (a) generate revenue, (b) plan for the desired operating profit, (c) have sufficient money remaining to meet the expenses required to generate the revenue, and (d) achieve all this without sacrificing quality requirements.

For a freestanding restaurant or other food service operation, the principles behind the determination of profit can be understood in terms of the accounting concepts of "return on investment" and/or "return on assets." Investors require that the property provide them with a reasonable return on their investment and that management safeguard the assets they have invested in the operation. This entitles investors to require additional profit to help compensate for the risk of their investment. In light of the high rate of restaurant failures, this risk is often great and, therefore, required returns are often high.

In lodging operations, investment requirements can be generated from the moms department, food and beverage department, and perhaps other revenue centers as well. The owner, working with the general manager, must first determine the amount of profit required from the lodging operation. Then, the staff must allocate profit responsibilities among the different departments based on expected levels of departmental revenue. The food and beverage manager will ultimately be responsible for generating a required amount of profit and will spread this responsibility between revenue-producing centers such as dining rooms, banquets, beverage operations, and room service.

Step 3: Calculate Projected Expense levels

Once revenue volumes are estimated and profit requirements are determined, expenses required to generate the projected level of revenue can be estimated. These expenses include: cost of food sold, labour expense, supplies expense, utilities, marketing expense, rent expense, depreciation expense, insurance expense, and many other expenses as well. Budget planning requires that management examine how these expenses are affected by changes in revenue volume. Fixed costs are costs that remain constant in the short run, even though revenue volume may vary. Common examples of fixed costs are: management salaries, rent expense, insurance expense, property taxes, depreciation expense, and interest expense.

Variable costs are costs that vary in relation to changes in the volume of business. If variable costs are strictly defined as costs that vary in exact proportion to arta revenue, then few costs, if any, are truly variable. However, several costs come dose to this definition and may legitimately be considered variable costs. For example, food and beverage costs increase as revenue volume increases simply because more food and beverage products must be purchased to prepare and serve the additional meals and drinks. Other examples of variable costs are labour costs for waged personnel and the cost of some supplies used in food production and service areas.

Mixed costs are costs that contain both fixed and variable cost elements. These costs are also referred to as semi-variable or semi-fixed costs. Although, in practice, the variable element of a mixed cost may not be directly proportional to usage or revenue volume, this assumption is generally accepted. An example of a mixed cost is telephone expense. One portion of this expense would be the fixed cost of the system, the other portion would be the variable cost of calls made during a specified period. Managers must consider each of these types of expenses as the budget is developed. The best method for estimating expense levels is, of course, the one that is most useful to the individual operation. Several widely used methods are described' in the following sections.

Simple Mark-Up Method

Perhaps the most common method of estimating food and beverage operating expenses is the mark-up method, which is based on the current expense level. This amount is then increased (or perhaps decreased, though this is rare) to arrive at the expense level for the new operating budget. For example, if the current month's food cost is $135,000, and a 12 percent cost (.12, as a decimal) increase is anticipated for the next budget period, the adjusted food cost for the new budget period is:

Budgeted food costs for each month are totalled to arrive at the estimated food cost for the new budget year. Total projected costs for the entire food and beverage operation are then determined by combining similar calculations for beverage and all other expense categories.

One problem with this method is that, by basing projections on current expense levels, it assumes all costs were reasonable during the current year. If in fact, some costs were too high because of waste, theft, or some other reason that inefficiency is extended into the new budget.

Percentage Method

Another frequently used method of estimating food and

beverage operating expenses is the percentage method, which is based on the percentage of each expense relative to revenue. Food and beverage cost percentages are calculated by dividing food or beverage cost by food or beverage revenue and multiplying by 100. The percentage method for forecasting food and beverage expenses assumes that the same cost percentages from the current period will continue to apply to the projected revenue for the new budget period. For example if the current beverage cost percentage is 24 percent, when the new budget is developed, 24 percent of the estimated beverage revenue is allocated for beverage costs. Like the mark-up method, the percentage method assumes that the current cost percentage is reasonable. This has the potential disadvantage of continuing an inefficient operation if the current budgeted cost percentage is higher than it should be. Close analysis to ensure that the budget allows for the planned profit goal can offset this disadvantage.

Zero Based Budget Calculations

A third method, zerobased budgeting, avoids the disadvantages of the other two by starting over from zero instead of extending costs or cost percentages transferred from the current period. This method takes more time and involves starting at a zero expense level for each category of cost and building up to new budgeted expense levels, justifying each step along the way. As a result, it yields expense information designed specifically for the period covered by the new operating budget. Forecasting costs in this way provides a very useful control tool for later comparing budgeted costs with actual costs. However because it requires a significant commitment of time to justify each cost estimate, the zerobased budget is not frequently used in commercial food and beverage operations.

Estimating Beverage Expenses

Separate costs for different beverage products may be considered in budget development. For example, suppose 70 percent (.70) of beverage revenue is estimated to be from liquor, and the beverage cost for liquor is 28 percent (.28) of its revenue. If beverage revenue equals $100,000, the total cost of liquor is:

% of Beverage Revenue X Total Beverage Revenue
X Beverage Cost = Total Cost

However, management must also consider the impact of other expenses such as labour, supplies, and advertising-on the entire budget. The same basic procedures can be used to estimate costs for all other expenses allocated to the food and beverage department.

For example, labour costs represent a significant expense for all types of food service operations. Managers must take the time to objectively assess likely labour cost levels based on estimated revenue. Energy and advertising expenses are other examples of costs that are generally significant and, therefore, demand attention during budget development. However, some categories of expense, such as office supplies, may have little financial impact on the food and beverage operation. Simple mark-ups are likely to be a fast and reasonably accurate way to budget for these expenses.

Computers and the Budget Process

Computers are now in common use for both routine and advanced budgeting applications in all but the smallest operations. The programmes designed to best per form these activities are termed electronic spreadsheet software. Electronic spreadsheets are simple in concept, but possess powerful computation capabilities.

Electronic Spreadsheets

Electronic spreadsheets resemble a traditional accounting worksheet since they are organised by rows and columns. The border along the worksheet's left margin typically contains numbers to designate row locations while the top margin contains letters depicting column locations. The intersection of a row and column forms a cell. A cell address is defined by its respective row and column indicators.

It is important to note that unlike an accountant's worksheet, which is very limited in size, electronic spreadsheets are stored in the computer's extensive memory. Spreadsheets are often so large that their size prohibits them from being displayed in their entirety on a display screen or monitor. At any point in time, the user views only a section, referred to as a window, of an otherwise enormous spreadsheet. The terminal keyboard contains cursor (arrow) keys enabling the user to move from cell to cell and from window to window.

Cell Contents

The food and beverage manager customizes a generic spreadsheet by defining the content of its cells. Electronic spreadsheet cells can contain a label, a number, or a formula. When textual information is entered into a cell it is referred to as a label. Spreadsheet software automatically identifies labels since they are entered from the terminal's typewriter keyboard. Labels assist in the organisation of data input and in the comprehensibility of output information. Headings, titles, chart of account lists, and the like typify budgeting labels.

Numeric values, used to produce calculated results, are entered into cells from the keyboard's number keys. The software is capable of identifying numeric input coming from the numeric keys) similar to the manner in which it recognises text characters for labels.

Formulas are preceded by special characters (for example, +) or words (for example, sum). These are used so that only the results and not the formula will appear in the addressed cell. Perhaps the most important benefit of spreadsheet software is its ability to maintain a formula that relates specific cells. For example, consider the spreadsheet below. Numeric values appear in cells B4, C4, 04, E4, B5, C5, OS, and E5. The results of stored formulas are presented in calls 07, E7, and B9. The formula used to produce the output in B7 is +B4 / B5. Cell C7 is generated from formula + C4/ C5. The calculated average food cost percentage found in B9 is computed from this formula: + B7 + C7 +07 + E7/ 4.

Formulas, capable of referencing various cells and constants, illustrate the usefulness of spreadsheet programmes. They enable someone who has only basic computer skills to direct the computational efforts of a powerful machine.

Recalculation Feature

The budgeting process generally requires many calculations. Moreover, whenever data is altered or extended, numerous recalculations are necessary. Spreadsheet software significantly enhances and streamlines this process since it contains for mulas composed of cell addresses and possesses a unique recalculation feature. Spreadsheets can be configured to automatically recalculate all numeric values whenever one value changes. Recalculations are performed in a chaining fashion. As a cell is modified, any and all cells related to it are also changed. In Exhibit 7, formulas in cells B7, C7, 07, and E7 relate corresponding row 4 and 5 elements. The formula in cell B9, however, depends on the calculated outputs of B7, C7, 07, and E7. Assume week two's food cost was erroneously entered.

The data in cell C4 should have been 3200, not 3000. When the cursor is moved to cell C4 and the figure 3200 is entered (replacing 3000), all subsequent computations dependent on this cell data (C7 and B9) will automatically be recalculated. In a manual process, these recalculations would require a working knowledge of the relationship among all data, and would take considerable time to accomplish. There would also be an increased opportunity for making errors in the recalculations. Budget reforecasting is becoming an increasingly used tool to help the food and beverage manager monitor the operation. The recalculation feature of electronic spreadsheet software enables food and beverage managers in all sizes and types of operations to quickly update budget projections by reforecasting revenue levels or expenses when necessary.

Food and beverage managers tend to appreciate spreadsheet output options as much as they do the usefulness of cell contents and automatic recalculations. Many electronic spreadsheet programmes provide both text (worksheet) and graphic output formats for any portion of the spreadsheet. Text output consists of a printed copy of me spreadsheet as it appears on the display screen.

The data on a spreadsheet can also be displayed graphically. Graphic options include bar charts, pie charts, or line drawings. Often, a visual presentation of the same data improves comprehension and understanding.

Cost-Volume-Profit Analysis

Cost-volume-profit (CVP) analysis is an analytical process used to determine the revenues required at any desired profit level. Also referred to as "breakeven analysis," CVP reviews the relationships among costs, revenue, and profits associated with alternative plans. CVP analysis is used to help managers answer such questions as:

— How many guests must the operation serve to meet budgeted profit goals?

— When fixed or variable costs increase, how many additional guests must the operation serve to meet budgeted profit goals?

— How profitable would it be for the restaurant to expand its hours of operation?

— Should the restaurant remain open during predictably slow meal periods?

— Graphs or equations can be used to conduct the analysis. Use of equations is likely to be faster and more accurate, and this procedure will be used in the discussion and examples that follow.

CVP Assumptions and Limitations

Like all mathematical tools, CVP analysis is based on several assumptions. If these assumptions are not relevant to the actual situations being analysed, the results of the analysis may be flawed. Some of the more basic assumptions behind CVP analysis include the following:

— Fixed costs remain constant during the period being analysed. Over time, fixed costs do change. However, it is reasonable to assume that fixed costs remain constant over a short time span.

— Variable costs vary directly with revenue during the period under study. In other words, if variable costs equal a certain percentage of revenue, and revenue increases, the new level of variable expenses will still equal the same percentage of revenue.

— Revenue relates directly to volume. For example, CVP analysis assumes that as business volume (the number of guests served) increases by a certain percentage, revenue will then increase by that same percentage. This means that decisions made from CVP analyses must be reviewed if, during the timeperiod in question, the sales mix changes. A change in the sales mix usually affects the amount of the guest check average. A higher average guest check results in higher revenue at the same level of business volume.

— All costs can be properly divided into two components: fixed costs (which do not change as revenue levels change) and variable costs (which vary directly with revenue).

— Only quantitative factors are considered by the CVP model. Qualitative factors such as employee morale, guest goodwill, and so forth are not considered. Therefore, food and beverage managers must carefully consider these qualitative factors before making any final decisions.

Basic CVP Equation

The basic CVP analysis equation expresses the cost-volumeprofit relationship at the breakeven point as follows:

Net Income (0) = Total Revenues - Total Variable Costs - Total Fixed Costs

Since there is no net income at breakeven, the value is set at zero when performing a breakeven analysis. However, the same equation can be used when an amount of desired net income is known. In these cases, the amount of desired net income is used as the value instead of zero. Variables within the basic CVP analysis equation can be broken down into the following more basic elements:

Total Revenues = Guest Check Average X Number of Guests Served Total Variable Costs = Variable Costs Per Guest X Number of Guests Served

Breaking these variables of the basic CVP equation into more basic elements allows managers the flexibility to rearrange the elements into new equations that address a number of different situations.

4

Menu: The Foundation for Food Costing

The menu is the foundation for the control process in a food and beverage operation. The menu planning control point begins the control process. Control points are basic operating activities that must be performed in any food service establishment. It also depicts the movement of servers from the kitchen to the dining room and the flow of food products from service staff to guests. (It is sometimes helpful to think of serving [moving the product from production staff to service staff) and service [moving products from service staff to guests] as separate tasks.

Beginning with menu planning, each control point plays a crucial role in determining the success or failure of a food and beverage operation. Each control point is a miniature system with its own structure and functions. Each basic operating activity has specific objectives, guidelines, standards, and internal processes that contribute to the success of the operation and the ultimate goal: guest satisfaction.

When a food and beverage operation is seen as a system of control points, the control activities associated with each function are easier to identify and carry out on a daily basis. This systems approach permits the manager to establish an audit trail of control activities. In short, the manager becomes proactive instead of reactive; that is, the manager takes time for short and long range planning in the hope of controlling future events, rather than waiting for crises to develop and then taking a "fire fighting" approach.

Process of Menu Planning

The process of planning a menu never ends; the final menu is never achieved. Rather, the process is ongoing, dynamic, and based on the expectations of the operation's present and potential guests-its target markets. From creating an image to communicating a plan for satisfying the guests, influencing the guests' purchase decisions, merchandising the correct products, and more, the menu has a continuous impact on all aspects of an operation. A properly planned and well-designed menu stimulates revenue and increases the guest check average, because whenever a menu is presented to a guest, a sales transaction begins. And the menu not only creates but also reflects the operation's image.

The image may be elegant, businesslike, fun, ethnic, or trendy, depending on what the target market(s) desire. The menu has an impact on every aspect of a food and beverage manager's job as well as the operation itself. The following sections identify some of the more important areas of a food service operation that are directly affected by the menu.

Product control procedures: The food and beverage products must be controlled. If an operation needs shrimp to produce a menu item, shrimp will need to be purchased, received, stored, issued, prepared, cooked, and served.

Cost control procedures: Careful cost, control procedures must be followed as more expensive products are served, as service styles dictated by the menu become more complex, and as guests desire a "dining experience," not just a " meal."

Production requirements: Food items required by the menu must be produced consistently. Product quality, staff productivity and skills, timing and scheduling, and other kitchen (back- or heart-of-the-house) functions are all dictated by the menu.

Nutritional content of meals: Non-commercial food service programmes and, increasingly, commercial food service operations are concerned about the nutritional content of food served to consumers. The menu can have an impact on the health and well-being of those to whom it is offered.

Equipment needs: Equipment must be available to prepare products required by the menu. The menu must be balanced based on available equipment resources so that no one station is overloaded or underutilised.

Sanitation management. Since the menu sets the stage for the remaining control points, management must consider menu items in light of possible sanitation hazards. Once the potential hazards are identified, the risks can be reduced.

Layout and space requirements. There must be adequate facilities for the staff and equipment required to produce items listed on the menu. The layout and design of facilities establish the physical space within which food production and service take place. The physical facilities must be adequate for the purchasing, receiving, storing, issuing, production, and serving of every item on the menu.

Staffing needs. Employees must be available to produce and serve all items required by the menu. As a menu becomes more complex, greater demands may be placed upon the staff. Staffing needs are also influenced by the degree to which the menu uses convenience food items (food items the operation purchases that require very little preparation).

Service requirements. The food and beverage manager must carefully plan how products will be served to the guest. The menu affects the skill levels required for service personnel along with equipment, inventory, and facilities needed in the front of the house.

Revenue control procedures. For example, when a simple menu is served in a fast-food operation, the potential for revenue control problems is not as great as the problem potential in a table service restaurant offering an elaborate menu.

MENU PLANNING

The menu is not only an important control tool, it is also a sales, advertising, merchandising, and marketing tool. In this respect, the menu addresses both control and marketing-related concerns and blends them into a workable system.

Marketing Implications of the Menu

Because it lists the items an operation is offering for sale, a menu, in effect, communicates a property's food and beverage marketing plans. In developing its marketing plans, a property needs to assess the products, service, ambience (theme and atmosphere), and perceived value that its target market(s) expect. Items selected for inclusion in the menu should be based on the needs and desires of the operation's target markets. In carrying out its marketing plans, the food and beverage operation must strive to meet or exceed the expectations of its target markets.

Management must never forget the marketing implications of the menu planning process. Notice that the most important and numerous concerns involve the guest and the quality of menu items. These are also the most complex concerns. Others include cost, availability, and production/ operation concerns. In addition, menu planners should study the competition and the types of menu items offered by both direct and indirect competitors in the area. It is especially necessary to consider items offered by competitors who are trying to attract the same target market(s).

Theme and Atmosphere

The complexity of menu planning in commercial properties depends upon the ambience of the food and beverage operation. Menu planning for table service restaurants is different from menu planning for banquet or buffet service operations. Ambience, the guests check average, and marketing concerns are prime examples of these differences.

Many food and beverage operations have a specific theme and atmosphere. French, Italian, and Chinese restaurants are examples of operations with ethnic themes. Others feature the cuisine of the American Southwest (for example, chilire-lenos, tortillas, enchiladas) or Cajun cuisine (for example, jambalaya, gumbo, blackened redfish). Still others create a healthy ambience by capitalising on an atmosphere and theme built on open, airy, plant-filled facilities that serve high quality, light, fresh foods. In any case, menu items offered must be compatible with the theme and atmosphere of the operation.

MENU PLANNING STRATEGIES

In the past, food service managers often attempted to

diversify their menus by adding many new menu items. Since most items were made from scratch, the number and variety of raw ingredients increased correspondingly. Another strategy, called" rationalisation," limits the menu to those items that best enhance the operation's image. Its objective is simplification for the sake of operational efficiency. An operation can offer several menu items that use the same raw ingredients. This cross-utilisation enables an operation to prepare and serve many menu selections with a limited number of raw ingredients.

When the menu is carefully planned to ensure a balance of menu selections in each category, the results of these new strategies can be a streamlining of the purchasing, receiving, storing, issuing, production, and serving control points. Today, as in the past, food service managers are searching for new menu item alternatives. The increasing number of highquality convenience foods has made it easier to offer new items without having to buy additional raw ingredients or elaborate equipment. Highquality convenience products can be purchased in semi-prepared or fully prepared forms. Because they have built-in labour, they also reduce inhouse labour requirements. Of course, convenience food products usually have a higher AP (as purchased) price than the raw ingredients from which they are made.

It is always best to base initial menu plans on the needs and desires of the target market(s). However, several other factors may influence the menu selection. Among these factors are the recommended storage conditions; personnel skill levels; the product's availability and seasonality; the stability of quality and price levels; and the operation's ability to purchase, produce, and serve the menu items in a safe, sanitary, and cost-effective way.

Menu Building

Entrees are typically selected first in the menu planning

process. It is important to consider not only the types of entrees, but also their costs, preparation methods, and compatibility with theme and atmosphere. A basic decision in planning the entree base concerns the number of entrees to offer. How many menu items should the operation provide? Some managers feel they should have something for everyone and, therefore, provide a wide range of entrees. This approach creates a number of problems that require careful planning and control to resolve.

The variety of entrees also affects the types and quantities of ingredients (each with its own standard purchase specifications) that must be received, stored, issued, produced, and served. A corresponding amount of preparation equipment and number of skilled personnel must also be available, and production/ service problems are more likely to occur. In summary, control is more complex.

The reverse approach of making available only a limited number of entrees reduces these types of problems considerably. In the United States there are many specialty/theme restaurants that offer relatively few entrees. By focusing on a specific segment of the market, this type of operation not only simplifies marketing techniques, but also minimizes many inhouse production, serving and control problems.

After selecting entrees, menu planners must choose menu items to complement the entrees. A common procedure is to plan appetizers and/or soups, followed by high-starch items and/or vegetables (if not part of the entree), then accompanying salads, and, finally, other menu components such as breads, desserts, and beverages. Trends in entree consumption affect the other items added to the menu.

Dining Trends

One dining trend compatible with many lifestyles is "grazing." Grazers are unlikely to select a full meal, but rather choose appetizers, salads, and desserts to complete their menu selections. Grazers are more likely to choose smaller portions of more menu items than to select a larger portion single entree. Therefore, menus featuring a wide selection of appetizers, salads, and desserts are popular with grazers. Menus are being designed with interchangeable courses, sometimes referred to as "modular cuisine."

The grazing trend is expected to continue and grow as guests change their eating habits and focus on the perceived high value of making multiple menu selections to "build their own" meals. The grazing trend seems to be particularly popular with the health- and fitness-conscious baby boomers, whose lifestyles reflect their desire for variety.

If a food and beverage operation's business is transient and the clientele changes frequently, the menu may be static (remain the same). Generally, menus that change-dynamic menus-are preferable to static menus. However, menu variability depends on the seasonal availability of raw ingredients at reasonable costs, the number and types of courses offered, the potential for using leftovers and local ingredients, the preferences of the guests, the operation's image, and the desires of the target markets.

When the business is highly repetitive and involves regular guests such as business people and others who reside in the local area, there is a greater need for daily specials that regularly change. Often, daily specials feature local or regional fresh ingredients and permit the menu planner to take advantage of reduced costs and increased availability to add interest to a menu. A trend today in daily specials is to announce their availability on attractive, eye-catching iridescent or colorfully lighted menu boards and suggestively merchandise them to guests.

Menu Design

The design of the menu can influence the guest's purchase decisions, stimulate sales of additional or preferable menu items, and increase the guest check average. Guests are influenced by visual cues provided by the menu. Readability, artwork, type styles, physical design, and layout play an important role in merchandising the food and beverage products that are profitable to the operation and satisfying to the guests. Menu items featured in these positions often draw the reader's attention because of their location. Of course, other devices such as art, pictures, and graphics can be used to draw the reader's attention elsewhere.

Menu Changes

Because conditions change, a food service operation's menu must also change. Menu changes are influenced by both external and internal factors.

External factors

External factors include consumer demands, economic conditions, the competition, supply levels, and industry trends. Consumer demands are perhaps the most important factor to consider in changing a menu. Management should first decide which potential markets it wants to attract with the modified menu. Then the proposed menu change must be evaluated in light of the negative and positive effects it may have on current guests.

Economic conditions include the cost of ingredients and the potential profitability of new menu items. Menu items offered by the competition may dictate choices to be made available. For example, a hotel food service located next to a restaurant offering the "best Chinese food in town" may elect not to serve Chinese cuisine. Supply levels relate the price to the quality and quantity of the proposed menu items. Supply levels are highly variable for some seasonal raw ingredients such as fresh fruits and vegetables. Industry trends provide general information about how the industry is responding to new demands. At present, an overall trend in many areas relates to a more sophisticated guest who is searching for an increasingly higher price-value relationship and who will pay more to receive more.

Internal factors

Internal factors that may result in a proposed menu change include the facility's meal pattern, concept and theme, operational system, and menu mix. The typical meal pattern is breakfast, lunch, and dinner. Management must decide if existing meal periods should be continued or altered. Expectations of guests have a direct influence on this decision. Any change must fit with the establishment's concept and theme. A restaurant that is known as the best steakhouse in the city may do itself a disservice by adding an extensive variety of fresh fish and shellfish to the menu. An establishment's image may also rule out certain foods that do not blend with its theme and decor. For example, even though ethnic foods are growing in popularity, a hotel restaurant may find it difficult to fit ethnic foods into its projected image.

Menu changes are also modified by the establishment's operational system. For example, if extensive new equipment purchases are crucial to the successful production and service of the menu item, the change may be too costly. Also, the change may raise both food and labour costs to unacceptable levels. Or, in some cases, the skill levels of production and service personnel may not be adequate to successfully produce and present the new menu item. The operation's existing menu has a certain overall combination or mix of items. This menu mix will be affected by any change in individual items. All of these factors should be evaluated before menu changes are finalised and implemented.

Calculating Menu Selling Prices

Commercial food service operations, as well as many institutional facilities, must establish appropriate selling prices for menu items. Objective pricing methods ensure that the property's profit requirements, as well as the value guests attach to the entire dining experience (including service, cleanliness, and ambience), are incorporated into the selling price. Pricing approaches examined are:

Subjective Pricing Methods

Although prices determine to a large extent whether financial goals of the operation are met, many managers use very subjective pricing methods. These methods establish prices, but generally fail to relate them to profit requirements or even costs. When the subject of pricing methods comes up, many managers speak about the" art" of pricing and suggest that intuition and special knowledge about guests' ability to pay are the most important considerations. Consider the following pricing methods and notice that each is based simply upon the manager's assumptions or guesses about what prices should be.

Reasonable Price Method

This method uses a price that the food service manager

thinks will represent a value to the guest. The manager presumes to know-from the guest's perspective-what charge is fair and equitable. In other words, the manager asks, "If I were a guest, what price would I pay for the item being served?" The manager's best guess in answering this question becomes the product's selling price.

Highest Price Method

Using this plan, a manager sets the highest price that he or she thinks guests are willing to pay. The concept of value is stretched to the maximum and is then "backed off" to provide a margin of error in the manager's estimate.

Loss Leader Method

With this plan, an unusually low price is set for an item (or items). The manager assumes that guests will be attracted to the property to purchase the lowpriced items and that they will then select other items while they are there. Beverage or food prices on some items are set low to bring guests into the property, but purchases of other items are necessary for the operation to meet profit requirements. This pricing method is sometimes used as an " early bird" or senior citizen discount to attract specific segments of the market.

Intuitive Price Method

When prices are set by intuition alone, the manager takes little more than a wild guess about the selling price. Closely related to this approach is a trial-and-error pricing plan-if one price doesn't work, another is tested. The intuitive price method differs from the reasonable price method in that there is less effort to determine what represents value from the guests' perspective.

These pricing methods are based on assumptions, hunches, and guesses. Such methods are generally ineffective because they do not consider profit requirements and the product costs necessary to put the item on the table.

These subjective pricing methods may be common in the food service industry simply because they have been used in the past, because the manager setting prices has no information about product costs or profit requirements to work with, and/or because the manager is not familiar with more objective methods. In today's market, with increased consumer demands for value in dining, and with higher purchase prices for products needed by the property, these plans seldom work.

Simple Mark-Up By Multiplier Pricing Methods

Some pricing methods use a mark-up by a multiplier based upon food costs for menu items. The methods are designed to cover all costs and to yield the desired profit. The following sections examine ingredients mark-up pricing, prime-ingredient mark-up pricing, and mark-up with accompaniment costs. Advantages and disadvantages of these methods are also discussed.

Ingredients Mark-Up Method

The ingredients mark-up pricing method attempts to consider all product costs: food costs when pricing food items, and beverage costs when pricing beverages. The three steps to pricing with this method are as follows:

— Determine the ingredients' costs.

— Determine the multiplier to use in marking up the ingredients' costs.

— Establish a base selling price by multiplying the ingredients' costs by the multiplier to calculate a final selling price.

A base selling price is not necessarily the final selling price. The simple output from formulas may not be an appropriate final selling price. Rather, a base selling price is considered a starting point from which other factors must be assessed and the price adjusted accordingly.

Prime-Ingredient Mark-Up Method

The prime-ingredient mark-up pricing method differs from the ingredients mark-up method in that only the cost of the prime ingredient is marked up. In addition, the multiplier used must be greater than the multiplier used when considering the total cost of all ingredients. Using the same oyster platter example, assume the prime ingredient cost is $2.65. If a multiplier of 5.02 is used, the oyster platter is priced at $13.30. The price is calculated as follows:

Base Selling Price = Prime Ingredient's Cost x Multiplier
$13.30 = $2.65 x 5.02$

If the cost of the oysters in this example increases to $2.75 for the dinner portion, the new price would be $13.81 ($2.75 x 5.02). The prime-ingredient approach assumes that the costs of all ingredients change in proportion to the prime ingredient. That is, when the prime ingredient's cost increases 10 percent, then other ingredients' costs are assumed to increase also by 10 percent.

Mark-Up with Accompaniment Costs

Using the mark-up with accompaniment costs pricing method, managers determine ingredient costs based only upon entree items and then add a standard accompaniment or "plate" cost to this amount before multiplying by a multiplier. This plate cost is an average cost for all non-entree and other relatively inexpensive items including salad, vegetables, bread, butter, and nonalcoholic beverages.

Determining the Multiplier

The mark-up pricing methods just discussed are simple to use and, for that reason, are commonly used in the food service industry. A significant disadvantage, however, involves determining the multiplier. How does a manager decide this? For many managers, it is a subjective decision based primarily upon experience and "rule of thumb" (such as the traditional 40 percent food cost). Should managers use last year's average food cost percentage? Should they use a statistic supplied by a national, state, or other food service association or consulting firm? It is, of course, possible to use a multiplier based upon the planned food and other costs from the operating budget. If, on the average, menu items are priced to yield the food cost percentage dictated by the budget, planners have developed a simple foundation for generating revenue sufficient to cover food costs and to yield a contribution margin (food revenue minus food costs) sufficient for other expenses and profit requirements.

The little time required to generate and use this multiplier based on the operating budget may make it especially cost effective for many small-volume operations. However, the impact of sales mix cannot be overlooked. If, for example, increased unit sales of a higher food cost percentage item replace sales of its counter parts with lower food cost percentages, the average food cost percentage can be made according to budget-but with undesirable financial results. There are other potential disadvantages of using simple multiplier pricing methods.

For example, these pricing methods do not reflect higher or lower labour, energy, or other costs associated with production of specific menu items. Rather, they either assume that all operating costs relate in some direct way to food costs or that these cost differences can be ignored. These assumptions may not be warranted as one considers the extensive amount of labour required to prepare some items relative to others.

The mark-up pricing methods using a multiplier also assume that all food costs associated with producing a menu item are known. In fact, many other costs may be excluded from the cost of ingredients used as the base for the multiplier. For example, operators not adjusting cost of goods sold by values of transfers to and from the food department would ignore these costs.

Contribution Margin Pricing Method

The term contribution margin refers to the amount left after a menu item's food cost is subtracted from its selling price. The contribution margin is the amount that the sale of a menu item" contributes" to pay for all non-food costs allocated to the food service operation and to help with profit requirements. With a contribution margin pricing method, managers can set base selling prices for menu items by following two steps:

— Determine the average contribution margin required per guest by dividing all non-food costs plus required profit by the number of expected guests.

— Determine the base-selling price for a menu item by adding the average contribution margin required per guest to the item's standard food cost.

Ratio Pricing Method

The ratio pricing method determines the relationship between food costs and all on-food costs plus profit requirements and uses this ratio to develop base selling prices for menu items. The three steps to ratio pricing are as follows:

— Determine the ratio of food costs to all non-food costs plus required profit by dividing all non-food costs plus profit by food costs.

— Calculate the amount of non-food costs plus profit required for a menu item by multiplying the standard food cost of the menu item.

— Determine the base selling price of a menu item.

The ratio method of menu pricing is simple to use and can be based on operating budget requirements. However, it does have several disadvantages. In an operation offering both food and beverages, it is necessary to separate non-food costs and profit requirements between the two revenue centers. Also, under this pricing method, each meal assumes an equal share of non-food costs and profit. The ratio pricing method does not compensate for higher labour costs associated with the preparation of laborintensive menu items.

Simple Prime Costs Method

The term prime costs refers to the most significant costs in a food service operation: product (food and beverage) and labour. A simple prime costs pricing method involves assessing the labour costs for the food service operation and factoring these costs into the pricing equation. The three steps to simple prime costs pricing are as follows:

— Determine the labour cost per guest by dividing labour costs by the number of expected guests.

— Determine the prime costs per guest by adding the labour cost per guest to the menu item's food cost.

— Determine the menu item's base selling price by dividing the prime costs per guest by the desired prime costs percentage.

The food cost for the menu item is the standard cost derived by costing the item's standard recipe. Labour costs and estimated guests are obtained from the approved operating budget. The desired prime costs percentage combines projected food and labour cost percentages, also from the operating budget.

The food service manager would then adjust this base selling price in relation to other factors, such as the operation's target markets and the competition. Advantages of this method are its focus on both food and labour costs and the fact that it is easy to use. An obvious disadvantage is the need to assign an equal labour cost to each menu item, even though the actual labour costs for menu items may vary greatly. The specific prime costs pricing method attempts to overcome this problem.

Specific Prime Costs Method

With the specific prime costs pricing method the food service manager develops multipliers for menu items so that the base selling prices for the items cover their food costs and their fair share of labour costs. Items with extensive preparation have higher labour costs and should have higher mark-ups. Conversely, items not requiring extensive preparation have lower labour costs that can be reflected in a lower mark-up.

The manager first divides all menu items into two categories: those that do and those that do not involve extensive preparation labour. The definition of extensive preparation labour is left to the manager to determine. For example, perhaps stew made from scratch is considered laborintensive to prepare, while a steak that only has to be broiled is considered non-laborintensive. Typically, all items are assumed to require approximately the same amount of labour for service and cleanup; these labour costs are shared by both categories of menu items.

Next, the manager allocates appropriate percentages of total food costs and labour costs to each category of menu items. Let's assume that the manager's analysis of menu items sold during a recent period showed that:

— 60 percent of the total food cost is expended for items requiring extensive preparation.

— 40 percent of total food cost is expended for items requiring little preparation.

— 55 percent of all labour costs is incurred for preparation of all menu items.

— 45 percent of all labour costs is incurred for service, cleanup, and other nonpreparation activities.

While the specific prime costs pricing method establishes base selling prices for the items to cover their fair share of labour costs, there are several disadvantages to this pricing method. Significant time may be spent in classifying menu items into extensive-preparation and non-extensive-preparation categories. Time will also be spent performing the necessary calculations. Also, this pricing method forces managers to assume that the relationships among all other operating costs vary in the same proportion as food costs. While this is often a reasonable assumption, there may be costs, such as higher energy costs, associated with preparing some items that reduce the accuracy of this method.

Important Pricing Considerations

The concept of value (price relative to quality) is always important. Guests pay for more than just the product (food and beverage) when they visit the operation. Quality of service, cleanliness of the facility, and atmosphere are also part of the dining experience and should, even if subjectively, be factored into the selling price decision. The basic law of supply and demand is another factor to be considered. Ultimately, the price that can be charged is established by the guests themselves as they decide whether to return to the property.

Volume concerns must also be considered. As fewer guests are served, overhead charges per guest increase;

selling prices must be higher. The reverse is also true: more guests may allow the manager to reduce overhead costs in the pricing decision. The price charged by the competition for a similar product is another concern. The more an operation can differentiate its products from those of the competition, the more freedom operation has in setting a selling price.

For example, perhaps two properties offer a similar steak dinner. While the price charged for the steak is important, there are other factors that may influence people to visit one property or the other. Perhaps one property provides entertainment, while the other offers an attractive atmosphere. Emphasising the differences between the property's own products and services and those offered by other businesses is one way to remain competitive.

One technique that can be used to attract guests from competitors is lowering menu prices. This may succeed in bringing more people into an operation, but only if the lower priced items are considered by guests as substitutes for what the competition offers. If there are no significant differences between what one operation offers and what the competition offers, then guests may see price as the determining factor in selecting one property over the others. However, if there are non-price-related differences that are important to guests (such as atmosphere, entertainment, etc.) this technique may not work.

Raising prices is also a way of responding to pressures from competition. With higher prices, fewer menu items will need be sold for the operation to meet profit requirements. However, raising a menu item's selling price may be effective only the increased revenue from the price increase makes up for the revenue lost as demand falls off and current guests begin to buy other menu items as substitutes. In fact, in some cases, more effective strategy for increasing total revenue may be lowering a menu item's selling price. Lowering prices may increase the volume of unit sales, and this increase may produce an increase in total revenue.

Menu Evaluation

You know the menu is a most important tool influencing the success or failure of food and beverage operation. The process of menu engineering is an increasingly popular approach to this problem of menu evaluation.

What is a "good" menu item? There are two measures of how good a menu item is: its popularity and its profitability. A popular menu item is ordered frequently by guests. A profitable menu item generates a high contribution margin. Menu items can be evaluated in terms of both their popularity and profitability. Basically, the menu engineering process uses information readily available to the food and beverage manager to classify menu items into four types:

— Stars-items that are popular and profitable

— Plowhorses-items that are not profitable but popular

— Puzzles-items that are profitable but not popular

— Dogs-items that are neither profitable nor popular

To classify each menu item into one of the four basic categories, managers must develop a practical way to define and measure the relative profitability and popularity of each menu item. This can be accomplished by using information about standard food costs and frequency of unit sales.

Some managers assume that the lower a menu item's food cost percentage, the more profitable the sale of the item is to the operation. In other words, the lower the percentage of revenue needed to pay for the food needed for the menu item, the larger the percentage of revenue available for all other expenses and profit. While this theory sounds good, it can be easily disproved.

Information about frequency of unit sales for each menu item can be gathered by tallying the number of each item sold during some specified time period (such as two weeks). This information can be abstracted from guest checks or, more frequently, by analysis of unit sales information from the electronic register or production records indicating leftovers, if applicable. Popular items are those with a relatively high menu mix percentage. Accordingly, "star" menu items are those with relatively high contribution margins and high menu mix percentages, while items classified as "dogs" score relatively low on both measures.

In performing a menu engineering analysis, it is not enough to consider menu items individually. Each item's contribution margin and menu mix percentage will provide measures for the item's levels of profitability and popularity, but the problem is to evaluate how high or low these levels are in comparison with all other menu items.

Profitability

The basis for measuring the degree of profitability of each menu item is the average contribution margin. A "high" contribution margin for an individual menu item would be one that is equal to or greater than the average contribution margin for all menu items. The concept of the menu's average contribution margin provides managers with a precise measure of each menu item's profitability, and it is easily calculated from readily available information. Recall that the contribution margin of a menu item is calculated by subtracting its food cost from its selling price.

Since the manager knows the costs incurred and the revenue generated for each individual menu item, the total menu costs and the total menu revenues generated can be determined by simply summing the figures for each menu item. The total contribution margin for all menu items is calculated by subtracting total menu costs from total menu revenues. Finally, the average contribution margin is calculated by dividing the total menu contribution margin by the total number of menu items sold during the specified time period in which unit sales data were collected. Individual contribution margins for each menu item can now be compared to the average contribution margin for all menu items to assess each item's level of profitability. A profitable menu item is one whose individual contribution margin equals or exceeds the average contribution margin.

Degree of Popularity

The basis for measuring the degree of popularity of each menu item is called the popularity index. This index is based upon the notion of "expected popularity." For the purpose of analysis, each menu item is assumed to be equally popular. This means that each item is "expected" to contribute an equal share of total menu unit sales. Therefore, the expected popularity of each menu item is calculated by simply dividing 100 percent (i.e., total unit sales) by the number of items on the menu.

Improving the Menu

The benefits of menu engineering can only accrue if information gained from the menu engineering analysis is used to improve the menu. What can a food and beverage manager do with this knowledge about the various food item classifications?

Managing plowhorses

First, let's consider plowhorses (those items low in contribution margin, but high in popularity). Guests like these items, but, unfortunately, plowhorses do not contribute their fair share of contribution margin. Possible strategies for managing a plowhorse menu item include:

— *Increase prices carefully.* Perhaps the item is popular because it represents a great value to guests. If prices could be increased, the item may still represent a good value, may remain popular, and may generate a higher contribution margin. This alternative may be most effective when the item is unique to the property and cannot be obtained elsewhere.

— *Test for demand.* If there is no strong resistance to price increases, it may be useful to complement an increased price with other strategies such as repackaging the item or repositioning it on the menu. These other strategies may be designed to maintain or increase the item's popularity while generating a higher contribution margin through the increase in selling price. If prices are to be increased, this should probably be done in several stages rather than all at once.

— *Relocate the item to a lower profile on the menu.* Depending upon the menu layout, certain areas of a menu represent a better location than others. A plowhorse can be relocated to a less desirable area of the menu. Since the item is popular, some guests will search it out. Others will be drawn to higher profile areas of the menu that list more profitable items the property wishes to sell.

— *Shift demand to more desirable items.* Menu engineering allows the manager to determine which items to sell-those high in popularity and high in contribution margin.

— *Combine with lower cost products.* The contribution margin of a plowhorse can be increased if lower cost meal accompaniments are offered with the entree. Perhaps, for example, higher priced vegetables and dessert accompaniments can be replaced with other, less expensive items without reducing the item's popularity. If this can be done, the contribution margin will increase.

— *Assess the direct labour factor.* The food and beverage manager should know if there is a significant amount of direct labour required to produce the plowhorse item. If an item with a low contribution margin does not have a significant amount of direct labour involved in production (a convenience food product, for example), the manager may be able to justify the lower contribution margin since fewer revenue dollars will be required to compensate for labour cost.

— *Consider portion reduction.* If the portion size is reduced, the product cost will be decreased and the contribution margin will increase. This alternative must be viewed with caution, of course, since the guest's perception of value may decrease when the portion size is reduced.

Managing puzzles

Puzzles are items that are high in: contribution margin but low in popularity-items the food and beverage manager desires to sell since their contribution margins relatively high. The challenge is to find ways to increase the number of guests ordering these items. Alternatives include:

— *Shift demand to these items.* Techniques include repositioning the items to more visible areas of the menu, renaming them, using suggestive selling techniques, developing advertising campaigns, using table tents, using buttons and badges on server uniforms, highlighting items on menu boards at the entrance to the dining area, and other strategies to increase the item's popularity.

— *Consider a price decrease.* Perhaps an item is low in popularity because it does not represent a value to guests. If this is the case, the selling price might be decreased with the contribution margin still remaining higher than average. This could lead to increased popularity, since a reduced selling price would represent a greater value to the guest.

— *Add value to the item.* Offering a larger portion size, adding more expensive meal accompaniments or garnishes, and using higher quality ingredients are among the ways that value can be increased. These techniques may lead to increased popularity and to a contribution margin that is lower, but still higher than the average generated by the menu.

Managing stars

Stars are items that are high in contribution margin and high in popularity. The best advice for managing stars includes:

— Maintain rigid specifications. Do not attempt to alter the quality of the product being served.

— Place in a highly visible location on the menu. Stars are items that the food and beverage operator wants to sell. Therefore, make sure guests are aware of their availability.

— Test for selling price inelasticity. Perhaps the star is popular because it is a significant value to the guest. Or, perhaps the star is not available in its existing form elsewhere in the, marketplace. These might be two instances in which the price could be increased without a decrease in popularity.

— Use suggestive selling techniques. Some of the techniques for shifting demand to puzzles might also be useful for stars.

Managing dogs

Dogs (items that are low in contribution margin find low in popularity) are obvious candidates for removal from the menu. After all, they do not contribute their fair share of contribution margin and they are not popular. Alternatively, the selling price could be increased, since this would at least generate a higher contribution margin. When ail dogll requires a significant amount of direct labour, does not permit sufficient use of leftovers, and has a relatively short storage life, the reasons for removing the item from the menu become more compelling.

The manager, guests, employees, and others may offer their opinions about the revisions. They may subjectively assess the menu's "worth" and offer their views about its improvements over earlier versions. By contrast, menu engineering can be used to evaluate menu revisions in an objective manner. For example, if the popularity of an individual menu remains stable (or increases) while its contribution margin increases, the revised menu is a good one.

Computer-Based Menu Management

While most automated food service management applications short and index data into timely, factual reports for management, menu management computer applications help management answer such question as:

— What is the most profitable price to assign a menu item?

— At what price level and sales mix does a food service operation maximise its profits?

— Which current menu items require repricing, retention, replacement, or repositioning on the menu?

— How should daily specials and new items be priced?

— How can the success of a menu change be evaluated?

Menu engineering is a menu management application that helps evaluate decisions regarding current and future menu pricing, design, and contents.

Menu Engineering Analysis

Data for analysis can be entered into the programme's database manually, automatically (from an integrated restaurant management applications package), or electronically (through an external ECR/POS system interface). A stand-alone version of menu engineering requires that the user input each menu item's product cost, selling price, and sales history. This minimal input is sufficient to generate a complete menu engineering analysis.

Food service operators who use computer-based recipe management applications to provide accurate product cost data can programme a menu engineering application to read this data from a file, rather than rely upon user input. Following data input and selection of the analysis option, the menu engineering application begins its work. As the analysis progresses, a menu item's contribution margin and unit sales activity will be categorised as relatively high or low. Procedures performed here are identical to those described for the manual analysis earlier. Eventually, each item will be further classified for both its marketing and pricing success.

Menu Item Analysis

This is an item-by-item listing accompanied by selling price, portion cost, contribution margin, and item count (number sold). The primary purpose of this report is to provide the user with a means by which to verify the data that is to be analysed. This can be helpful when data has been manually entered into the programme.

Menu Mix Analysis

The percentage of menu mix (%MM Share) is based upon each item's count divided by the total number of items sold. Each percentage is then ranked as high or low depending upon its comparison with the menu engineering rule for menu mix sufficiency. The percentage each item has contributed to the menu's total contribution margin is found in the column labelled % CM Share. Each item's contribution margin is then ranked according to how it compares with the menu's weighted average contribution margin (ACM).

5

Menu Engineering

The term menu engineering refers to the specific restaurant menu analysis methodology developed by Michael L. Kasavana, Ph.D and Donald J. Smith at the Michigan State University School of Hospitality Business in 1982. Menu Engineering is the process of using a marketing assessment to help generate additional gross profit from a restaurant's menu.

Understanding Menu Engineering

By using guest demand (also called the menu mix) and gross profit margins, the relative performance of each menu item is determined, and assigned one of the following terms:

Stars

Stars are extremely popular and have a high contribution margin. Ideally Stars should be your flagship or signature menu item

Plow Horse

Plow Horses are high in popularity but low in contribution margin. Plow horse menu items sell well, but don't significantly increase revenue.

Puzzles

Puzzles are generally low in popularity and higher contributions. Puzzle dishes are very difficult to sell, but are have a high profit margin.

Dogs

Dogs are low in popularity and low in contribution margin. Basically they are difficult to sell and when you do they are not all that profitable. Several variations to this methodology have been developed at hotel and restaurant schools around the country which have had qualified results.

Over the years, the term menu engineering has become a buzzword within the industry which has come to mean "doing something/anything to improve menu performance", slang for the generic use of the term. In the hands of a skilled practitioner, menu engineering can be a powerful tool which points out a wide range of strategies and tactics which can lead to large increases in the profitability of restaurant menus.

Menu engineering looks at the sales history, selling price, and cost of food for menu items. It relates their profit or contribution margins and their menu mix percentages to determine which items are both popular and profitable.

Percentage method

The cost as a percentage of sales method is shown below. You determine what percentage of sales food costs should be. A price is calculated by dividing the cost by the established percentage, which in the sample is 30%. You can update prices by checking the box to the right of a particular item and clicking 'Update Prices'.

Contribution method

The 'Contribution Method' refers to the contribution that the sale of each menu item should make toward covering the production costs and profit. Profit, when using this method, is to be treated as an expense that is to be covered by sales. The amount is calculated by dividing profit or Total Contribution (Gross food sales - Cost of food sold) by the number of customers.

BOTTOM LINE SOFTWARE

Perhaps the oldest misconception in foodservice management is that food cost is directly related to profitability. In other words, the lower an operation's food cost percentage (food cost divided by food sales), the more profitable the restaurant is assumed to be. This simply is not always the case.

Menu Engineering Software

While most foodservice software applications are primarily concerned with controlling and manipulating numbers, menu engineering deals with decision making strategy. Menu engineering is a deterministic approach for the evaluation of current and future menu pricing, design, and content decisions.

Menu engineering software focuses attention on: a) customer demand (number of covers sold), b) menu mix (sale preference scoring), and c) contribution margin (gross profit). The model provides both a menu item and overall menu analysis for competing menu items, by meal period. It establishes a benchmark against which future menu changes can be evaluated.

Percentages certainly serve as important managerial controls by providing feedback that cannot be otherwise obtained. The menu engineering concept requires that management orient itself to the number of dollars a menu contributes to profitability, not to merely monitoring cost percentages. Menu engineering software goes beyond traditional valuative approaches by assisting operators in obtaining a reasonable level of profitability through increased customer demand and/or increased average contribution margin per menu item.

Menu Engineering Model

Menu engineering begins with an interactive analysis of menu mix (MM) and contribution margin (CM) data. Competing menu items are categorised as high or low gradients according to MM and CM achievement rules. A menu item whose MM is greater than or equal to 70 percent of its equal menu share is considered high, otherwise it is labeled as low.

Menu Engineering Application

Data for analysis can be entered manually into the software's database, automatically from an integrated software module, or electronically via an external system interface. A stand alone, off-the-shelf version of menu engineering software requires that the foodservice operator be familiar with each menu item's product cost, selling price, and number sold. This minimal input is sufficient to generate a complete menu engineering analysis.

Since restaurateurs may employ recipe costing packages, designed to more accurately provide product cost data, menu management packages can be configured to retrieve this data from a file, rather than rely on manual computation and/or input. Similarity, selling price and number sold data, already captured in a point-of-sale (ECR/POS) system, can likewise be transmitted to a menu engineering package for processing. Obviously a foodservice establishment employing both integrated software and interface capabilities will experience a minimal amount of data preparation and handling during the course of a menu engineering session.

Menu Prices And Food Costs

To keep food costs in line, it is important to have consistently in portion control. Ingredients are purchased in weight, count and volume. Calculate the cost of all ingredients used in the production of a specific menu item (the actual item, seasonings, garnishes). Total these costs and divide by a food cost you wish to achieve for that menu item. This determines a menu price.

The Factoring Method - Multiply the cost of ingredients by three (this method does not include labor or other costs)

Gross Margin Pricing - The formula is gross profit minus cost of goods sold divided by net sales. A gross profit margin of 0.33:1 means that for every dollar in sales, you have 33 cents to cover your basic operating costs and profit. This is a good method for dishes having a high cost of ingredients.

Prime Cost Method - The formula is to add the cost of labor and cost of food, add a percentage for profit. This method is good for dishes that require a lot of preparation.

Competitive Pricing - Competitive pricing seeks to match what others charge for the same product or service. Conduct a market study and compare the prices to similar ones on your menu. That means pricing your product neither very far above or below what others charge.

Combination Pricing -This method considers all methods, factoring, gross margin, prime costs and competition, and tries to balance the prices of the competition with your costs and needs.

Software

ChefTec Software - Designed by an executive chef and a staff of programmers for food-service professionals. ChefTec lets you customise management reports and print out recipes, organise monthly inventory procedures, generate ordering lists and maintain your par levels. You can instantly analyse recipe and menu costs by portion or yield, update prices and change ingredients in every recipe.

Chef Office - ExecuChef started as a simple way to organise vender orders, value inventory and cost & scale recipes.

PC-Food II is a food costing, inventory and margin management system for use in restaurant, catering and all food service operations. Calculate and maintain food cost and required selling prices based on desired margin. Edit portion sizes and ingredient costs to see the effect on costs and margins. User selectable sorted displays and reports. Unlimited departments, export ingredients to file, up to 30 ingredients per recipe, up to 30 ingredients and/ or recipes per menu item. Three levels of recipes (recipes may use other recipes). Also calculates total revenue, food cost and gross profit for a banquet, etc. Available option to change currency symbol. PC-FOOD II also maintains inventory quantity and value. PC-FOOD II then calculates the ending value at the latest cost.

CostGuard - A tremendous inventory, recipe, menu, food costing and pricing tool. Software for food service operations: restaurants, hotels, institutions, corporate, B&I, clubs, caterers, retail, and educators.

Menu Development and Analysis

Menu is one of the important aspects for the success of any foodservice establishment. Perhaps it is arguably the soul of the restaurant. Menu infers several interpretations for both the buyers and sellers. Khan suggests that "menus are statements" of the food and- beverage items provided by a foodservice establishment, primarily based on consumer needs and/or demands and designed to achieve organisational objectives". Mooney and Kreck note that menu can be interpreted as a list of product range that a restaurant offers and the same time it can be a piece of literature or display used to communicate the product range to the customer. However, a recent study argues that "menus are more than the conventional function of a communications and selling tool but also a research and experimentation device that can be studied to increase restaurant profit".

An interesting point is that the battle for pre-eminence menu offered to the consumers is an endless task faced by most foodservice operators. A matter of fact this process is actually an endless cycle of research and analysis because once a new menu is developed that menu is periodically reviewed for its effectiveness. Quite simply, the research process is crucial to find out what is going on in the market and the analysis process determines which dishes need further assessment. It is this periodical review known as menu analysis that determines the success of the menu performance.

In broad terms, menu analysis can be defined as a range of techniques and procedures that enable more effective decision making both with respect to marketing and operating the menu. Various tactical solutions to menu analysis have been sought in endless attempts by many restaurant operators to improve menu performance.

Subsequently more tactical solutions to menu analysis have emerged. The issue of non-material variable costs, which is claimed being ignored in the previous menu analysis approaches, becomes prevalent of its important in the works of Hayes and Huffman, Bayou and Bennett and LeBruto et. al. respectively. Other approaches such as the micro-marketing mix and economic approach have each advocated their own method of tactical solutions to menu analysis. Although all these menu analysis approaches advocate different tactical solutions for analysing the menu items' performance, they all share the same objective, which to improve (or to provide a solution for) the current menu items performance.

Research Methodology

A qualitative approach was undertaken to ascertain chain foodservice attitudes in the menu analysis decision-making. Although the acceptance of qualitative research methodology is less prevalent than the quantitative research, it is argued that the choice of qualitative research would fulfil the needs of the purpose of this research project. Quite simply, the interest of this research is a phenomenological approach, an approach to understanding how menu analysis is conducted by foodservice operators rather than the use of a positivist approach, which is largely based on measurable variables and provable propositions.

This qualitative research approach to inquiry also involved a case study approach, where people and setting were explored in-depth and described in a series of mini-case studies reports. It is believed that a series of mini case studies reports would enhance the body of knowledge in understanding the intended research objectives. Thus, personal interviews were deployed to explore the phenomenon of interest from the foodservice operators with the use of a semi-structured questionnaire, which was composed based on the secondary research and piloted in predetermined sampling settings.

Undoubtedly, a large-scale population would make this qualitative case study research more valid and reliable. However, to conduct in-depth personal interviews in a large-scale survey would be too costly and time consuming. This to a large extent answers why a case study approach was adopted in this qualitative research. Mass financial capabilities and diversification of divisions and departments provide huge advantage in making the operations more efficient and effective. Furthermore with the increased numbers of outlets, a need for better menu analysis methodology is surely crucial apart from being competitive in the market.

To a large extent, the variables that needed to be measured were quite complex and subjective because most of the different approaches to menu analysis advocated different criteria and each of them function differently. Some of the menu analysis approaches have incorporated tangible and intangible elements to advocate their menu analysis techniques. Because of this, 'statistical generalisation' or enumerate frequencies' were considered unsuitable, instead 'analytical generalisation' or 'expand and generalise theories' was a more appropriate selection of measurement.

Quantitative Approach

The findings show that the obvious equipment used by the chain operators to analyse the menu performance is the Electronic Point-of-Sale (EPOS). Almost all of these chain companies have an advance computer system, which is linked with the EPOS. Because of this the menu analysis is entirely conducted in the head office and such analysis from the EPOS at the restaurant outlets are no longer applicable.

Quantitative data analysis is predominantly the main method to assess the menu mix sales volume popularity) and gross profit profitability/ contribution margin). The findings imply that once the new menu is launched in the market, the first criterion used to review the menu effectiveness is the menu sales mix reports. Daily sales mix reports are accumulated for a period of one month to produce a monthly sales mix report. Every menu item sales volume and gross profit are analysed and the outcomes of what actions should be done for the menu items are decided in several ways.

However, this quantitative data analysis is not the sole determinant to decide what actions should be done to the menu items. Other criteria such as based on intuition, experience and company's financial policy are also taken into considerations for appropriate alternative approaches. This seems to confirm Jones's propositions where he argues that 'menu changes.. .are based on strategic decisions rather than simply on analyses of operating performance (and) the addition and removal of a new menu item is often based on competitive and market analysis". Details of these alternative approaches are explained under sub-heading: alternative approaches to simple and complex menu analysis.

Qualitative Approach

Qualitative analysis approach is indeed equally important as the quantitative data analysis for the chain operators when a menu analysis is conducted, specifically deciding what actions should be done for the menu items. Endless research projects are carried out to analyse customer trends in food preferences and acceptances. These research projects are vital to supplement information for menu development so that improvement for new and current menu items in term of its value and nutritional acceptances, taste, ingredients and presentation can be enhanced.

The analysis of customer trends is obtained in many ways. The findings reveal that market analysis is the common method used to obtain the plausible answers of customer trends. Analysing the target market disposable income and age population, competitors menu and awareness of current issues in food preferences and acceptances is the main areas of concern in the market analysis. Apart from this market analysis, travelling to Italy and French, which known of their gastronomic expertise is visited regularly to seek popular dishes that suitable for UK market, particularly in London market.

Based on intuition and experiences rather than relying detailed quantitative analysis are also played crucial part when a menu analysis is conducted. It should be remembered that most of these chain companies have been established for many years therefore, decision on how to analyse, amend and develop the menu items is largely based on previous experiences. Because of this, many of the chain operators analyse their menu items by advertised its on the black board menu, popular radio channels, and relevant magazines.

Customer feedback such as complaints, suggestions and compliments about the menu items are crucial for the success of the menu efficiency. Sometimes low popularity and profitability of menu items may not cause by diminishing of customer demands but poor control of the food production is likely be the culprit. Because of this, mystery shoppers are assigned to analyse the menu performances in term of its quality, presentation, taste, and the waiting period after the order taken. The accumulative of this crucial information is indeed the 'source of aspirations' for the chain operators to act what amendments and developments should be done for the menu items.

Menu Analysis Conducting

The findings appear to disclose that the prevalent methods of how menu analysis is conducted by chain operators are combination of qualitative and quantitative analyses. Notably, quantitative data analysis is the dominant approach used by chain foodservice operators when analysing the menu mix. The use of sales mix reports generated by EPOS is the main source of inputs to analyse the menu mix performances.

Sales volume popularity and gross profit profitability/contribution margin) are the common criteria under investigation for every menu item. In addition, the use of gross profit percentage (GPP) is also found to be adopted. Although different methods are used to measure menu effectiveness, some of the methodologies used by the chain operators to analyse the menu item popularity and profitability seem corroborated with the theoretical menu analysis approaches. Nevertheless, none of the theoretical methodologies of menu analysis are totally embraced by the chain operators.

Apart from using the quantitative data to analyse the menu performances, the use of mystery shoppers is also adopted to analyse the menu performances in term of its quality taste, value and overall presentation. Additionally, periodical inspection of food production processes are also conducted by the chain operators for making sure all standard procedures are followed according to specification. The finding implies that these analyses are indeed very essential so that the generation of the sales analysis produces more accurate and reliable information.

After the menu analysis is completed, the next stage is to determine whether the menu items should be modified or not. Based on the theoretical menu analysis approaches, clear guidelines of what solution should be done for the menu items are demonstrated. Unfortunately, there is no definite evidence emerged in the findings in term of which criteria used to decide whether the menu items should be modified or not. Furthermore, the decision to ascertain which alternative approaches should be taken for the menu items is somehow varied from one chain operator to another.

For example, one of the chain operators is hardly relied on the sales analysis, instead the company's President experiences in products improvement (modification) is the main source for decision-making. Unlike, other chain operator, the menu items are analysed comprehensively and it involves more than one person/ department. Yet, the decision to ascertain which alternative approaches should be taken for the menu items is still pending on the market research and customer trends.

Thus, the decision making to decide which appropriate approaches to be done for the menu items is quite complex and it involves various persons / departments. Nevertheless, regardless of which decision the chain operators decide to base on, several alternative approaches are highlighted based on the findings of the case studies, which can be the ideal solution. Detail explanations of each of these alternative approaches are presented below.

Alternative Approaches to Simple Menu Analysis

There are four alternative approaches, which fall under the 'simple menu analysis'.

— Promotion,

— Re-position,

— Retention and

— Elimination

From the analysis, it is found that the main reasons why the foodservice operators are declined to modify the menu items composition are because of the following criteria:

Menu promotion

Promotion is used to analyse further the menu effectiveness because experiences and marketing strategy indicated that lack of awareness from the public eyes may be the caused why the menu items are low in demand. This strategy is adopted because the result of low popularity obtained from the sales analysis may not be necessary due to loss of customer demands. Sometimes the demand of the menu items is still alive but lack of public attentions can cause the faith of the menu items in jeopardy therefore, every precaution should be observed before the menu items undergo such modifications. Menu promotion involves both internally and externally. Black board menu and mini table standing menu, which highlights 'problem dishes' only, are the example of internal promotion. On the other hands, using popular radio channels, posters and fliers in busy places such as cinema, hybrid places, etc. is the notable findings in their external promotions.

Menu repositioning

Changing the presentation and layout of the menu design is quite essential for boosting the menu sales. A matter of fact, this is one of the dominant approaches used to boost the sales of low popularity menu items by placing them at the strategic location known to be in the centre of the menu. These findings can be linked to the works of Miller, where, according to him, menu items that most want to sell should be placed above the middle on a one-page menu. The analysis carried out on respondents' responses has revealed that placing the items at the wrong position can cause an adverse effect of its demand. Because of this, the result of the sales analysis to some extent can provoke incorrect decision on what solutions should be taken for the menu items. Additionally, proper choice of words uses to describe the dish ingredients and methods of cooking also played a part for improving the menu popularity.

Menu retention

Undoubtedly, successful menu performances in term of its popularity and profitability should be retained. There is nothing to do with these menu items except to maintain or/and improve its quality in order to increase the popularity. However, an interesting finding obtained is that any menu items, which are known as 'problem items', are still being retained in the menu. Nonetheless, the composition of these items is subjected to be reviewed and modification is likely to be implemented.

Subsequently, once these three options are finalised and implemented, the menu items will undergo to menu analysis again. In fact, the review of menu effectiveness is an ongoing process mainly because of the changes in customer demands. It is these changes in customer demand, which make the menu items to be reviewed periodically. Needless to say, the ultimate aim is to detect the 'shadow of customer demands' (which either be high or low) before it happened.

Thus, the use of sales analysis to measure the menu effectiveness to correlate with the alternative approaches as to improve the item performance is insufficient. A matter of fact, using market analysis and customer feedback to detect customer trends and correlates with the alternative approaches as to improve the items performance is more convincing than the sales analysis. These findings probably answer the reason why the theoretical menu, which uses hard data to analysis menu item performance as to improve the item popularity and profitability, is problematic.

Menu elimination

There are several reasons why decision is made to eliminate the menu item. Menu items that are no longer popular properly due to menu fatigue and changes of customer preferences and acceptances such as healthy foods are the real caused why the menu items are eliminated. Limited supplies and escalating in product prices are also found to be the caused for menu items to have been eliminated. An interesting point emerges that decision making to eliminate menu items is predominantly based on qualitative analysis rather than from the sales analysis.

Introduce new menu items

Decision to introduce new menu items is mainly because of customer demands. The most common sources referred by the chain foodservice operators when considering to add menu items into the menu are company's research and development department (R&D), market information from Mintel and Keynote reports and Henley Data, professional hospitality journals and customer feedback. It should be remembered that the addition of menu items can only be materialised after thorough analysis from market demands. Moreover, current kitchen equipment and personal expertise about the new dishes are also due consideration in the internal analysis. Finally, the new menu items are launched in the market and the process of measuring the menu items effectiveness begins again.

Alternative Approaches to Complex Menu Analysis

There are five alternative approaches, which fall under the 'complex menu analysis'.

— Presentation,
— Re-price,
— Re-costing,
— Modify recipes and
— Reposition

These notable alternative approaches used by the chain foodservice operators to modify the menu items composition. The finding reveals that most of the chain operators make the decision to modify the menu items based on the actual performance against the predetermined criteria and allow the menu items to be further developed as appropriate. In this case, menu items which fall below acceptable level are bound to be undergone such modifications. Unfortunately, details of the 'acceptable level' are somehow quite ambiguous. It appears that there is no definite time period when the menu must be changed or modified after the launched of the menu. Regardless of how frequents the menu items are modified, here are the alternative approaches adopted by chain operators as to improve the current menu items performance.

Menu items presentation

The main references that are used to decide the modifications of the menu items presentation are mystery shoppers and the customers. Customer feedback such as complaints and suggestions are essential for improving the menu items presentation. However, what form of research instrument are used to seek customer feedback is not mentioned. The author suggests that an "informal procedure" is likely to have been adopted where such feedback is reported on a random basis based on the recollection of staff experiences. Unlike the mystery shoppers, there are more formal and standardised, and independently performed by outside foodservice consultant. Depending on this feedback analysis, the presentation of the menu items may be modified either one or combination of these elements: taste, garnishing, saltiness, colour, texture, etc. Nevertheless, the use of chefs artistic expertise in food presentation also plays a part in decision making for menu items presentation.

Menu re-pricing

Usually, such decision to re-price the menu items is caused by several factors. The finding indicates that inflation is the main caused why chain operators re-price the menu items. Another factor that contributed to menu re-pricing is because of over-pricing the menu items. For example, one of the operators says that over-pricing the menu items could be the main reason why the demand of such items declined and not because of the deterioration of the foods quality or demand. When the selling price is changed to slightly low than the former one, the popularity of the menu items has increased by 5 percents.

In addition, unavoidable factors such increase in distribution costs and liquor tax imposed by the Government also lead to re-pricing the menu items. Of course, other considerations such as company financial policy, food costs and pricing strategies are also contributed to the changing of the selling price.

Menu re-costing

An obvious finding show that the cause of re-costing menu items is highly correlated with the change of the product specifications. Any changes on products purchase price from the suppliers therefore, leads to the change of the standard specifications. Notably, the standard specifications are designed by the menu planners which than becomes the control tools for menu recipes and portion size. Simply put, any modification on the items' presentation is indirectly caused its recipe specifications to change. Thus, any changes involve between these factors will lead to menu re-costing. Apart for that, the change of the item portion size also leads to menu re-costing. Above all, many chain operators have allocated a budgeted food costs by the Finance department for every chain's outlet for cost control purposes. Hence, any chains' outlets that are found to have been exceeding the budgeted food costs that outlets' menu items cost will be reviewed and menu re-costing is subsequently followed.

Recipes modification

Recipe modification is basically linked with the menu re-costing.

Menu re-positioning

Unlike the menu repositioning discussed earlier, this part discusses those menu items that involve several modifications from its name, recipe, selling price and presentation. The findings reveal that after the menu items undergo several modifications (depending on how many menu items are modified) new menu design is developed with high probability of changing the menu layout and general presentation of the menu card, since the former menu card is no longer applicable with the modifications being made. Thus, the applications of the menu repositioning discussed earlier are being used again. However, if only a small proportion of the menu items undergone such modifications than the menu items may go for promotion or repositioning.

Launch Revised Menu Item(s)

Subsequently, after the menu items undergone such

modifications regardless of which alternative approach is used these revised menu items are reviewed of its effectiveness again. Similar procedures of menu analysis discussed above are applied and the processes of how menu analysis is conducted begin again.

How to Price Your Restaurant Menu

Writing the menu for your restaurant is the fun part. It's kind of like picking out names for a baby. You can play around with terms and pair different foods together to see what looks good together. However, a menu, just like a new baby, can be rather complicated and hard to understand at times. For example, how do you know what to charge in order to make a profit? Food cost and portion control are two ways to help price your menu correctly, so you make a profit but be careful not to price yourself out of the local market. Another way to ensure a profit is to create a balance of expensive and inexpensive items.

Food Cost

Food cost refers to the menu price of a certain dish in comparison to the cost of the food used to prepare that same dish. In other words, how much you pay for food will determine how much you need to charge for it. Generally, food cost should be around 30-35%. This means that if you pay $1.00 for something, you need to charge minimum of $3.34. It may seem like you are charging a lot more than necessary, but keep in mind that you aren't just paying for the food itself. You are paying someone to prepare the food, serve the food, and clean up after the food. Everything in your restaurant, from payroll to the electric bill needs to be covered by the food you serve.

Portion Control

One reason that chain restaurants are so successful is that they have a firm handle on portion control. The cooks in those restaurants know exactly how much of each ingredient to put in every dish. For example, shrimp scampi may have a portion control of six shrimp per dish. Therefore, every shrimp scampi that goes out of that kitchen will have six shrimp in it, no more, no less. This is portion control.

In order to practice portion control in your own kitchen, everything should be measured out. Chicken, beef and fish should all be weighed, while shredded cheese can be stored in portion control cups and a measuring cup can dish out mashed potatoes. Once you feel comfortable cooking your menu, you can eyeball the serving amounts but in the early stages of your restaurant, err on the side of caution and measure everything out. Another way to practice portion control is to purchase pre-portioned items, such as steaks, burger patties, chicken breasts, and pizza dough. They may be more expensive, but can save you money in labor and food waste.

Well Balanced Menu

Food markets fluctuate depending on the season, the weather and the price of gas. One day lettuce may be $10.00 a case and then the following week it has jumped to $30.00 a case. There is little you can do when prices jump, short of changing your entire menu every few weeks, and who has time for that? However, when you balance expensive items, which are prone to price fluctuations, with items that have stable prices, you can help maintain your desired food cost.

6

Pricing of Food Products

A product cost is a subtotal of all the money you spend to make, package, promote and distribute the food products, combined with the costs to operate the business. A good set of business books will make this step much easier and more complete. Once you know the complete product cost and the volume produced, you can figure how much it costs to make each unit.

Be sure you include all costs in your product cost subtotal. If you plan to use a retailer or distributor, remember a typical margin over your price is 40 per cent. For example, you have found a specialty store retailer who is interested in stocking your sage jelly. The store requires a 40 per cent margin and will price the jelly at \$2.49 per jar. Can you cover your costs and make a profit at \$1.49 per jar? The formula to calculate selling price is:

$$\text{Selling price} = \text{cost} \times \text{factor}$$

$$\$1.49 \times 1.667 = \$2.49$$

When you know the selling price and the margin you can calculate your price by using the following formula:

$$\text{selling price} \div \text{factor} = \text{cost (or price)}$$

$$\$2.49 \div 1.667 = \$1.49$$

Mark-up Equivalency Table

Margin %	*Mark-up %*	*Factor*
30.0	42.9	1.429
31.0	45.0	1.450
32.0	47.1	1.471
33.0	49.3	1.493
34.0	51.5	1.515
35.0	53.9	1.539
36.0	56.3	1.563
37.0	58.8	1.588
38.0	61.3	1.613
39.0	64.0	1.640
40.0	66.7	1.667
41.0	70.0	1.700
42.0	72.4	1.724
43.0	75.4	1.754
44.0	78.5	1.785
45.0	81.8	1.818
46.0	85.2	1.852
47.0	88.7	1.887
48.0	92.3	1.923
49.0	95.9	1.959
50.0	100.0	2.000
60.0	150.0	2.500

Product costs include both variable and fixed costs. Most of your expenses will fall into three categories.

MATERIALS

Include all material and supply costs, such as raw ingredients and packaging, used to make your processed food products. Material expenses are variable costs. Each time you spend money to make a product you increase your variable costs. To identify variable costs, look to see which costs keep pace with the amount you produce. When you make twice as many samosas in your commercial kitchen, your variable costs will double.

Example: A processor of dilled carrots would include the costs for jars, carrots, seasonings, vinegar, labels and the shipping costs in the materials cost group.

Labor Costs

The amount you pay the people who make your food product should be added to labor costs. Remember to include a cost for your own labor. If you are unsure how much time you spend working on production activities, keep track for one week in your daytime calendar. Labor costs for machine operators and any people who prepare the food product, package or prepare it for shipping. Most labor costs are variable costs since they change with the number of units made.

Overhead

Business expenses such as facility and equipment expenses, insurance, utility costs, depreciation and salaries for management are overhead costs. You could also be paid for your management activities, as well as your labor. If you can't directly trace cost to labor or materials, it likely belongs in overhead. All overhead costs are fixed costs. Fixed costs are a part of operating a business. They can't be tied to the number of units produced as they are the same whether 10 or 10,000 are produced. You have to pay your fixed costs whether or not you sell anything.

Example: Liability insurance protects your business if someone is injured while visiting your place of business or by consuming your product. This is an overhead cost. Product cost is an important first step in setting product price. It tells you the minimum amount your product can be priced. You need to know your product price before you can calculate how many units you must sell to break-even. The break-even point is where there is neither a loss nor a profit from the sale of your products. Once you know product cost you can use customer and competitor analysis to further refine your product price. The worksheet attached to this factsheet walks you through this process.

Break-even point: A good product price strikes a balance between costs, volume and profits. You can use a break-even calculation to see whether costs are covered by a certain price and volume.

Break- even analysis can also help you analyse how a price change affects your business. From the worksheet, you can find out how much of your product you have to sell to cover your product costs. If you can't sell enough to cover all of your costs, you have to adjust your selling price or reduce your expenses.

To earn a profit you must add it to the break-even point. The break-even calculation tells you where total revenue equals total cost. If you set price or volume below the break-even point you will lose money each time you sell your product. Price or volume above the break-even point will ensure profits.

To calculate the break-even point you must know your fixed costs, variable costs and unit contribution margin. To calculate contribution margin you subtract variable costs from the price. Use contribution margin to experiment with various prices before you settle on a final food product price.

Contribution margin is a quick way to figure how much fixed costs each unit can carry.

Unit contribution margin = unit sales price–unit variable cost

Example: Happy Cheese Company produces a spiced Camembert cheese for \$1.20 per 100 gram variable cost and sells it to a wholesaler for \$2.00 per 100 gram

Unit contribution margin

$$\$2.00 - \$1.20 = \$0.80$$

This means each Camembert cheese produced can pay \$0.80 fixed costs for the company to break-even.

Break-even point in units =

$$\frac{\text{Fixed costs}}{\text{Unit contribution margin}}$$

Example: Happy Cheese Company has \$1,000 in fixed costs for the spiced Camembert cheese.

$$\text{Break-even in units} = \frac{\$1{,}000}{\$0.80} = 1{,}250$$

To make no profit, but cover all the costs at \$2.00 per 100 gram, Happy Cheese Company must sell 1,250, 100 gram packages of cheese.

To achieve a target profit or target operating income for the business use the following formula:

$$N = \frac{\text{Fixed costs} + \text{target profit}}{\text{Unit contribution margin}}$$

Example: Happy Cheese Company wants to generate \$1,000 target profit

$$N = \frac{\$1{,}000 + \$1{,}000}{\$0.80} = \frac{\$2{,}000}{\$0.80} = 2{,}500, \text{ 100 gram pks.}$$

To earn \$1,000 profit for the business, Happy Cheese Company needs to sell 2,500, 100 gram packages of cheese.

Profit Goals

Every business needs profit goals to set direction and to ensure the business not only survives, but thrives. To set a profit goal you must consider cash flow needs, product position and family member business goals. Profit goals project how much profit your food processing business should earn. You can set your profit goals as a percentage above the product cost subtotal or set a total profit figure for the entire business. A profit goal guides decisions on the amount of product you make and the price you charge.

The product position of your food products should be linked to profit goals. Product position describes how target customers view your products. Do your customers at the farmers' market think your chutney is high quality, unique and worth the extra trip? If so, you can charge more for your chutney. This affects the amount of profit you can earn.

Example: Happy Cheese Company is in its second year of operation. It plans to expand its marketing strategy next year. A profit goal for 1999 is to earn $1,000 monthly.

Marketing of Products

Direct Marketing

People who sell their products directly to the consumer are direct marketing. To ensure success in direct marketing you need to do some research. You need to research how your product compares to the competition, the demand for your food product and the unique benefits.

There are many types of direct marketing:

Farmers' markets

A farmers' market is a focal point where producer and

processors gather on a regular basis to offer home-grown produce, agricultural and home-crafted products to sell directly to consumers. All Alberta approved farmers' markets operate under rules and regulations implemented by Alberta Agriculture, Food and Rural Development. Individual farmers' markets may also have additional rules and regulations. The theme is, "Make It, Bake It or Grow It."

The advantages of using farmers' markets are direct contact with a larger, regular and loyal customer base, lower marketing and overhead costs, greater income and a market to test new products. The disadvantages are extra time away from the food processing business, possible low sales volume and the costs to transport product to the farmers' market.

Trade shows or trade fairs

A trade show is an efficient way to market your food product to the hospitality and food service industry. It's also a great way to network with firms specialising in equipment, financing, training, quality control and promotion. ARFEX is an annual trade show alternating between Edmonton and Calgary. The trade show is sponsored by the Alberta Restaurant and Food Service Association (ARFA).

A trade fair provides feedback from industry experts and an opportunity to market products to the wholesale gift marketplace. Uniquely Prairie is a four-day show, held in Edmonton during August in conjunction with the Alberta Gift Show. Written feedback is given to all participants in Uniquely Prairie. Comments are made by experts in merchandising and marketing who rate products on design, workmanship and saleability. Products with a judge's recommendation are given space in a special creative arts display space where they receive extra information and coaching on display management.

Gift baskets and mail order sales

This type of direct marketing works best for non-perishable products such as dried fruits and vegetables, preserves, flavoured vinegars, spices and candies. The main advantages of gift basket and mail order sales are they aren't location dependent, they appeal to a new customer base and they provide collaboration opportunities with other food processors to create unique product combinations.

Food service or door-to-door sales

When you take your processed food products to peoples homes, retail businesses, institutions and restaurants you are in the door-to-door sales business. You can also work with a worthwhile charity to sell your food product to help raise funds. Business owners like this type of direct marketing as it has low overhead costs, easy entry and exit, and no location requirements. The disadvantages include legal restrictions, licensing requirements and image problems related to quality.

Farm gate sales

If your farm has plenty of parking space and is easy to get to, it may be ideal to encourage customers to come to the farm. To offer on-farm sales you need a cash register, weigh scale and perhaps a cooler, depending on your product. On-farm sales offer lots of flexibility on length of season, size, hours of operation and product mix. The advantages of farm gate sales are on-site location, a broad range of products, year-round employment and additional income. The disadvantages include extra capital for buildings, finding and keeping reliable food product suppliers, and the need for a good location. Check to be sure you comply with municipal or provincial regulations regarding zoning, health, safety and primary and secondary highway road allowance right of way boundaries.

Other types of direct marketing you could use to sell food products include home parties, a web page and telephone selling.

Indirect Marketing

When you use an indirect market you place one or several market channels between your food product and the customer. You may decide to use an indirect marketer for the following reasons: less time commitment, an expanded customer base and lower capital requirements. Examples of indirect market channels are wholesalers, retailers, institutional buyers and brokers.

Wholesaler

A wholesaler pays for your food product and owns the goods. Most wholesalers have invested in buildings and capital. They are able to store large volumes of food products and may even repackage goods to meet the needs of various customers. The wholesaler earns income by reselling your food products in mixed lots or smaller quantities to retailers or institutions. Example . Happy Cheese Company is a new business and has decided to use a wholesaler so it can focus on producing high quality Camembert products.

Retailer

Some retailers buy food products directly from you and sell them to the consumer. This practice is very common among small one-store retailers or very large retailers who have invested in storage facilities and transportation. Specialty retail shops are a good example of a small retail operation as they prefer unique, locally made products. Use several types of retailers to diversify your food product portfolio and to expand your sales.

Institutional or foodservice buyers

Examples of institutions that might buy your food products are schools, hospitals, hotels, nursing homes and military bases. The larger institutions often find it more cost effective to buy directly from food processors and absorb the transportation costs, rather than purchase it from wholesalers.

Broker

A food broker provides an expert sales force, local representation and stable sales costs. Some of the tasks a broker can do for your business include: representing your product, visiting stores regularly, monitoring product sales, handling complaints, pulling product or rushing unplanned orders. Many brokers also handle any special promotions or displays you request and monitor competitor activity. Fees for brokers range from three to 10 per cent (commission).

The commission fee is negotiated along with fees for special services such as the planning of promotions or data collection. To find a broker ask five or six retailers which brokers they use and why they like them. When you interview a food broker, take along some facts such as a product description, suggested retail price, shelf life, the type of packaging used and the amount you can supply. Plan to discuss fees, major clients, experience with the product category and the five largest retailer accounts they handle. You need to know if the broker has a conflict between your product and other products they currently market.

International Marketing Options

Most business advisors recommend that you have a good domestic customer base before you consider marketing internationally. However, you may decide to develop a product exclusively for an international market. You may also know someone who has detailed knowledge of a foreign market and is prepared to help with the groundwork.

There are some good reasons to consider an international market. Provided your food product is priced properly, an expanded market should increase profits. International markets offer a larger and more diverse market base, can extend the life cycle of your food products and can give you more security through diversifying into different global economies. It's crucial for you to develop a market focus if you are considering an international market.

Marketing internationally also has major risks. You need to consider the costs of foreign currency exchanges, cultural differences and the need for additional market research. International marketing is a long-term commitment requiring up-front capital and patience. It's a good idea to prepare a short list of countries you are interested in exporting your food product to. Before you select an international market, remember to research trade barriers, tariffs and taxes, market size, the degree of competition both domestically and from foreign operations, the distribution network and political issues.

Advantages of Marketing Methods

— *Direct marketing* — lower marketing costs, larger customer base and increased,income potential
  - — able to earn more profit on products you sell
  - — a market to test new products

  - direct contact with customer
- *Indirect marketing*— some indirect sellers are more cost effective and efficient due to economies of scale
  - buyers and sellers are linked together very efficiently
  - some types of indirect sellers take responsibility for marketing your product
- International marketing—expanded markets can increase profits
  - can increase and diversify your customer base
  - less chance of sharp sales decline if selling to many different economies

Disadvantages of Marketing Methods

- *Direct marketing*—additional time required to sell products
  - may need additional capital for buildings
  - if transporting products to customers will have extra costs
  - need to comply with legal restrictions and licensing requirements
- *Indirect marketing*—adds an extra cost to your product
  - lose contact with the customer if you sell through indirect channels only
  - you may find there are few indirect sellers interested in distributing your product
- International marketing—need to manage foreign currency exchange, cultural differences and additional market research
  - need patience to invest capital and wait for return on investment

Price Strategy of Competitors

When you research competitors you are taking an industry focus. An industry focus goes beyond considering your costs of production. It's comparing your business products and strategies to those of your competitors. The more you know, the better decisions you can make about products, price and strategy.

Step 1 — Prepare a main competitor list

It's important to narrow down the competitive field to main competitors, otherwise the price range may be too large and inappropriate to your business. To learn more about competitors you can conduct a secondary data search or ask customers or suppliers for their opinions.

Step 2 — Analyse the main competitors

Ask customers how they feel about the competition. Tour competitors' businesses to learn how products are priced, packaged and distributed. Find out how competitors have reacted to price changes in the past. Prepare a list of the strengths and weaknesses of your business. Compare it to your main competitors.

Step 3 — Welcome customer complaints

Make it easy for customers to tell you what needs improving. Customers will tell you how your price compares and what you can improve. Once you ask customers what you can improve, be sure you take steps to correct the problems or customers will feel they were ignored. Include your customers in market research as they are often well informed.

Step 4 — Assess if new competition will enter your market

Most industries are open to new entrants and you should

expect more competition. Constantly check with customers, suppliers and your competition to see if they have heard of any new businesses. A quick scan of trade journals such as Specialty Foods, Gourmet Retailer, Prepared Foods or Canadian Grocer will help you to discover new businesses similar to your own.

Step 5 — Discover where the competition is selling

You need to find out which stores purchase goods from the competition, and why. Try to find out if the competition offers other types of reductions or price cuts to buyers.

Step 6 — Observe trade show activity

If your competitor sells through trade shows, assess how their prices and sales volumes compare to yours.

Customer Demand for Product or Service

Demand level describes how badly the customer wants your food product and what they will pay. To assess the demand, you need to know the size and nature of your customer base and the customers feelings about price. The more you know about your customer group, the easier it is to design product price. To learn more about the demand for your food product(s) you will need to answer many questions, such as:

— How many buyers are there and where do they live?
— How old are your customers, how much do they earn and what is their education level?
— What size and type of family does customer have?
— How does your customer like to spend money?
— What do your customers do in their spare time?

— Does your customer believe price indicates the quality of a product?

Research will help you find the answers to these questions. There are two types of market research, primary data and secondary data.

Primary data provides original, tailored information about the wants and values of your customers. Target customers are asked carefully worded and sequenced sets of questions. The answers are analysed to find out more about customer attitudes towards new products, pricing, packaging, distribution and marketing. Most business owners find they must hire a market research professional to design the primary data questionnaire and to interpret the data.

To conduct informal primary research on your food products, start by listening to your customers. Question your customers about pricing, service, quality and new food products. Invite your customers to fill out customer comment cards or brief questionnaire forms. Use this information to evaluate customer attitudes towards your food products and prices. Primary research asks target customers for their opinions and ideas. You can also tailor primary research to learn more about your competition and what target customers like most about your competition.

More elaborate primary research includes written surveys, telephone interviews, focus groups or person-to-person customer interviews. All research projects should begin with a secondary data search. To learn more about target customers and their attitudes toward pricing, you can check Statistics Canada, the Business Development Bank of Canada (BDC), Dun and Bradstreet reports, trade magazines, government newsletters and the internet. There are many types of trade magazines that can provide information, intelligence and contacts in the food processing industry.

Understanding how to price your processed food product is an essential step in developing your business. You must continually monitor your price including your costs of production, your competition and your customer. You must also be prepared to make adjustments. In competitive businesses, the successful product is the one that can change quickly and continue to operate profitably.

7

Liquor Costing

Inventory, pricing, keeping liquor locked at all times, proper training etc., are the tactics of managing liquor cost.

Conduct Inventories

If you feel you have a high liquor cost, liquor inventory can be done on a nightly basis. Keeping a perpetual inventory of bottles is a great idea. Bottles of beer and wine can be balanced each night. Since the cost of liquor and the price being charged varies across the country, it is difficult to say what a good cost is and what a poor cost is. Targeted goals are as follows:

— Liquor cost: 23%

— beer cost: 25%

— wine cost: 35%

These may vary depending on your state and location of your restaurant. In South Carolina, the liquor cost will be higher because they are still using mini bottles! Contact you state restaurant association for the average cost in your area.

Use a gigger to measure liquor when making drinks. If you believe in "freehand" pouring, properly train using exacto pours and conduct pour tests with your bartenders on a daily basis prior to each shift.

Have a system in place the requires your bartenders to ring each item as they are made and that each customer has a accurate total of his or her bill.

Have a system in place that allows your bartenders to buy drinks for the customers. This will reduce their need to steal from you, while building business at the bar.

Do not let your employees sit at the bar after their shift or even on their nights off. There are many reasons for this, such as the possibilty of free drinks being given away, losing seats for bar guests, employees getting tanked and creating an overall unprofessional atmosphere.

Pricing

Check pricing and make sure all you employees are chargin the correct amount for each product.

Depending on your state, work with your liquor vendors for case deals and reduced pricing for large orders.

Managers should check in all orders to maintain accuracy of pricing and product being checked in as well as eliminating the possibilty of theft from your driver or employee who may be checking in the order.

Put Controls and Systems in Place

1. *Determine actual usage by taking regular inventories.* This should be done at the same time, same day every week to ensure that the trends reflect accurate usage.
2. *Set up pars for all bars and liquor storage locations.* A "par" is the amount of product necessary to sustain business for a specific period of time. This is also the level to-order-up-to. For a storeroom this should be set at a level that would be sufficient for the busiest

week of business for that particular season and the amount to last until the next order. The par for specific locations, such as "the main bar", should be set at a level that would be sufficient for the busiest single day of the week. It is common to have different pars for different seasons. Have pars set up for each station in the bar. Pars should be posted so that every bartender/manager knows what should be there.

Set your storeroom par with AccuBar—Pars are important for several reasons: 1) Pars serve as a guideline by which to order product, 2) Pars insure that you do not run out of product, 3) Pars in each bar location will help you identify if something is missing, and 4) In case someone new or inexperienced must place the order they will then have something to go by (sooner or later you need a vacation.)

3. Invest in a computerised point-of-sale system that will allow you to track sales, comps & voids by item, time and by employee.

Ordering

4. Never let a salesperson or the bartender determine what your order should be.
5. The same person should place the order each week because they form a relationship with the sales rep and generally have the best understanding of product usage and the cost structure.
6. Monitor and track weekly liquor usage to determine a usage trend that the store normally goes through. Watch for variances to that trend.

   Practice "Just in time" inventory control. As a rule, order only what you will need to get through one week, so that new product is received just in time as current product is used up. If you must order more to realise a "price break" or to save the extra "broken case" cost, do so only if you will go through the additional product in a normal accounting cycle of approximately 1 month. Otherwise factor in the cost of carrying the product versus the amount you will save. Try and maintain a MINIMAL level of product in stock.

7. Only order products that compliment the concept. Ask yourself "Is this product likely to bring in new customers? Or, will this product build sales with existing customers? Better yet ask yourself, "If I do not have this product will I lose customers or lose sales? If the answer to the latter question is no, then you probably do not need the product. Beware of salesmen that "need a favor" or "need a placement". Don't bring in products that you will have to hold a "fire sale" to get rid of later down the road. Look on your shelves and see if you have any of those "hot new products" from 8 to 12 months ago. Carry only those products that compliment your concept, your sales and satisfy your customers. Keep it simple.
8. Remember the season and upcoming events. Is there anything special or larger than normal quantity that needs to be ordered?
9. Check with the sales representative for special pricing or up-coming price increases. They will usually be willing to give you the inside scoop on upcoming sales, discounts or changes in the industry that might affect quantity/quality/pricing. If your rep does not do this then you may consider requesting a new rep.
10. Place the order using product codes, so there are no surprises.
11. Make sure that the perishables are being ordered appropriately. You can track the usage by day as well.

Receiving

12. Take the order guide or "purchase order" with you when you receive deliveries. Verify the invoice to the order guide to insure that what is ordered is what is delivered. It is common that a salesman may "up" the order to make their quota.

13. Check in and sign for all deliveries. "Never sign for a delivery if you did not personally check it in. (This is especially true for the Chef and the food deliveries.) Go through each case that is delivered to make sure that it contains what the invoice says.

    Check the "quality" of the delivery, before the driver leaves. Check all open cases to ensure no bottles are broken, chipped, or otherwise unacceptable. Check that the produce and perishables are in good shape and will be fresh for usage.

    Keep a Credit Log. Follow up immediately for any credits that are owed. If they do not adjust the bill upon delivery, request a faxed copy, the next day. If any merchandise is unacceptable have the driver write it on the invoice and initial. You do the same. Write it on your credit log.

    If the driver comes during a busy time (lunch 11 - 2pm) tell them to come back. It is a bad habit to accept a delivery at a time you are "normally busy". The driver will then expect you to accept orders at their convenience.

    If a driver gets mad, abusive, or refuses to come back, Call their Supervisor. If the problem persists request a new driver. If the invoice has product listed that was not delivered the driver must write what was missing on the invoice and initial. You should do the same.

STORAGE AND LIQUOR STOREROOMS

14. Lock the inventory away immediately. Never let anything sit out.
15. Immediately log the order on the perpetual. The perpetual will provide a running count of what is on hand in inventory and the current inventory carrying cost.
16. Put the delivery away immediately. Plan for deliveries and schedule yourself enough time to check it in, organise and put it in the proper storage area.
17. Never leave the liquor room open for an "hourly" to put things away, (and never toss the keys to an hourly to put open the liquor room storage area.)
18. Make sure that the storage room/walk-in/freezer is safe, so that bottles can't fall and break, product will not spoil, etc... Fix that broken or "leaning shelf" before it costs you money to replace broken product.
19. Ensure that product is rotated, such as; beer, wine, and perishables. Practice FIFO (first-in, firstout).
20. The liquor room should have a self-closing auto-locking mechanism. This means that the door will swing shut and there is no way to turn the lock to an "off" position.
21. The beverage requisition should be out and used in the liquor room, along with the perpetual. Otherwise use the "bottle-in, bottle-out" method. In other words, if a bottle must be pulled from the liquor storage area during a shift, then an empty bottle must be left in its place.
22. If refills are needed during a shift, follow a "bottle-in, bottle-out" system, only giving a full bottle for an empty bottle. If bottles are transferred from one bar to another, the main bar must bring the empty bottle

of Chivas in exchange for another bottle of Chivas. If bottles are exchanged with the liquor room, leave the empties in the liquor room.

23. Breakage and requisition of bottles should follow a four-part check-and-balance system.
    1) The closing bartender lines up all "broken" or emptry bottles and writes them into a requisition sheet at the end of each day. The closing bartender signs.
    2) The closing manager verifies that what is being requested is what is "broken" or empty at the end of the that shift. He/she then counts the empty bottles by type and checks off the requisition sheet. The closing manager signs. Closing bartender can then toss empty bottles.
    3) Opening manager pulls the new bottles from the storeroom to fill the requisition and delivers new bottles to the designated bars. The opening Manager then signs the filled requisition.
    4) The opening bartender accepts the requisitioned bottles and puts them away in the designated places in the bar. Then the bartender verifies that all bottles are "on par". The opening bartender signs the completed requisition.
24. Deface the empty bottle with a box cutter or permanent marker and ensure that all empty bottles are discarded in the trash and are not re-used the next evening as "false breakage".
25. There should be plenty of Store n' Pours available. These should be color-coded or have labels that identify the contents. Also, use day dots or production tags for homemade mixers like Bloody Mary mix etc... "

"Behind the Bar"

26. Make sure that every area where liquor will be unattended is secured. Lock it up. Everything should be locked up every night. This includes cranberry, apple juice etc...
27. Prep only enough bar consumables for the shift. Watch out for the bar back who cuts two gallons of limes regardless if it is Friday or Monday.
28. Label the stations within the bars to designate where the each liquor bottle should go. This makes it easier to notice when something is missing.
29. Rotate coolers and reach-ins nightly. Old comes out, new goes in back, and the old goes back infront. This helps ensure FIFO.
30. Eliminate employee munching. Limes/lemons/bananas/cherries are expensive.
31. Consider a policy that all employees pay (a nominal price) for bar consumable products, namely juices. If they want cranberry juice or orange juice they must pay for it and be able to show a receipt.
32. Make sure that the bar staff follows ringing procedures (Silent System). They should never to talk to the bartender unless explaining an odd request. If everything is an "odd request" then they may need more training.
33. Track "wasted", spilled or deleted items to track "lost opportunity costs". If possible use the POS system to appropriately ring and record these transactions. Consider this example: A strawberry daiquiri was ordered and made. The guest changes their mind and now wants a piña colada. They are the same price. Ring the wasted daiquiri on the POS to track the loss. Also make sure those drinks do not find their way to an employee's lips.

34. The cocktail & food servers and bartenders must know all the different types of liquor and how to ring them up accurately. This will decrease wasted drinks from server error. They should review their check before sending it. Review their void & waste lines when collecting "server cash-outs". If high, document it in a memo.
35. Quiz the bartenders on specs. Do they know how much rum is in a "rum & coke"? Do this weekly if possible. Have the specs handy. Have them do pour tests with dummy water bottles.
36. Conduct bar drawer audits. It is like a mid-shift, mini-cash out. Use the element of surprise. Try one per week per manager. The time of day should always be random.
37. Spot-check a minimum of 5 tables/tabs per employee per shift.
38. Have the bartenders put the purees and syrups in a pan with appropriate ladle size. If the recipe calls for 2 oz of strawberry syrup for a strawberry margarita then make sure the bartender is using a 2 oz ladle.
39. Use measuring scoops for ice. Never dip a glass into the ice as it can chip and leave glass fragments in your ice bin. This causes drinks to be returned, customers to get upset, downtime to "burn the ice", and possibly even a costly law suit.
40. Make sure employees have adequate supply of glasses and supplies. If they are constantly running out of things they will become frustrated and may become less caring. They may also think that the manager is not watching things very closely.
41. Track keg, box or tank usage. Mon closing = 12 Gallons, Tues AM should = 12 Gallons. Use a hydrometer for tanks.

Hands-on Management

42. Periodically check to be sure that the POS has the correct prices and that the manager's codes have not been compromised.
43. Make sure that all boxes are crushed before going out to the dumpster. Beer boxes for example: An Open box = Empty box = Crushed box = Dumpster. An "empty uncrushed box" may = "full bottles" of something heading toward the trash but ending up in someone's trunk!
44. Practice proper, clear and regular communication between all managers. Never allow employees to hear managers bicker between one another. Likewise a manager should never complain about another manager to an employee.
45. Check all prices against the invoices and the vendor pricing guides.
46. Make sure that the accounting procedures are organised.
47. Use contests to ensure good bartender practices such as reduction of blender waste or meeting projected liquor costs. Share expectations and results.
48. Have the bartenders make their own action plan for correcting high cost areas.
49. Have the managers make up an action plan for high cost areas.
50. Hold staff meetings regularly to communicate expectations and review problem areas. Also, solicit good ideas and input from employees. Reward employees who are meeting expectations.

8

Food Cost Analysis

Even if your actual food cost percentage was as good as your planned one, it does not mean that you have achieved your best performance possible in the food cost area. Keep in mind that the actual food cost percentage is nothing more than the combined result of many factors. Some of these factors may have been negative while others may have been positive.

Efficient Food Cost Performance

It is a basic fact that the profit margin in any food operation does not allow room for inefficiency, whether it is in the food cost, labor cost, or expense. In other words, inefficiency may force the food operation to close down. Therefore efficient performance in the food cost area is paramount. Every dollar you save in food cost will turn out to be an extra dollar in profit. The following equation is a typical and simple statement for any food operation.

Food Sales - [Food Cost + Labor Cost + All Other Expenses] = Profit

Efficiency in Food Cost Percentage

A statement such as "you do not take a percentage to the

bank" or "you can't pay bills by percentage" does not undermine the simple fact that food cost percentage is the only tool available today to evaluate and measure the performance in the food cost area. The food cost percentage can be defined as *"the relationship between food sales dollars and food cost dollars."*

Acceptable Food Cost Percentage

Unfortunately there is no such magic number, simply because there are four variables that must be considered when deciding an acceptable food cost percentage for the operation.

As indicated in table 1 below, all three operations were successful and achieved the same bottom line, yet they operated differently from each other to achieve such profitability. Take for example, the B operation in comparison to the A operation. The B operation had planned and accepted a higher food cost by purchasing more partially or fully prepared food items and their trade-off is lower labor cost by not having to trim, peel, or cut as much in-house.

On the other hand, the C operation had planned and accepted an even higher food cost percentage in comparison to the A and the B operations and their trade-off is to reduce the other expenses such as live entertainment.

As you can see, an acceptable food cost percentage for any one operation is nothing more than the percentage that will create the perfect balance among the four variables that affect the food operation—namely menu price, food cost, labor cost, and other expenses. Simply put, what is a suitable food cost percentage for one operation is not necessarily suitable for another.

Tabel 1. Food Operations

Operation	*A*	B	C
Food sales (In 000.)	100	100	100
Less			
Food cost	25	30	35
Labor cost	35	30	30
All other Exp.	15	15	10
Profit (L.)	25	25	25

Becoming Efficiency in the Food Cost Area

It is important to emphasize that efficient performance in the food cost area does not mean blindly cutting costs regardless of the effect it might have on the quality and quantity of the food served. In fact, this will most likely end up having a negative impact on the food cost, especially in the long run.

The only way to actually achieve an efficient operation in the food cost area is by implementing the following cycle:

Planning: In this stage, the decision makers will choose—after studying the market, the clientele, the type of skills, and equipment available—what type of menu will be served. Target goals are then set in each of the four variables, namely menu prices, calculating the food cost potential, the dollars to be spent on labor, and all the other expenses.

In planning the food cost target, a recipe sheet is prepared to identify and calculate the type and amount of ingredients required to produce every item on the menu. Management will cost and price these items, then calculate the food cost potential. The food cost potential (also known as the planned food cost, the ideal food cost percentage, or what the food cost should be) can be defined as "a calculated target, tailored for a particular operation, attainable under certain assumptions (prices, expenses, people skills, equipment, etc.) to produce at the end of the cycle (purchasing, receiving, storing, issuing, producing, and serving) the desired return on investment." In other words, a planned food cost percentage is that which will produce, with the other factors, the desired results for the operation. Staff training and several other issues are covered in this stage.

Control: Once the operation starts, management needs continuous feedback about the performance, not only in the food cost area, but also in all other activities. The feedback needed by management is only possible with good internal controls which can be defined as "all the measures taken by the operation such as policies, procedures, and systems, etc. to safeguard the resources against error, fraud, and inefficiency." For example, in the food cost area you will find that policies and procedures such as the use of daily quotations and order forms are a must, all food suppliers must be approved in advance, buying should be within the approved specifications, the executive chef must sign all food purchase orders or requisitions, items received should be checked, counted, and weighed, etc.

The system should produce steady, timely, and accurate data about performance as well. Obviously the amount and type of controls will depend on the size of the establishment, the experience of the people involved, and the type of system and equipment in use. In a small operation the owner or the manager can rely on visual supervision and there is no need for costly and complicated controls. The larger the operation, the more sophisticated the controls will be.

Analysis: Sometimes the type of information produced by the system is either not enough or needs to be broken down further. Sometimes the data needs to be measured in relation to other data. During this stage, management will be able to identify the problem, its size, what caused it, and ultimately how to rectify it.

Corrective Actions: Management must act as soon as the feedback reveals any inefficiency. It must take the necessary steps to tighten control over the operation and improve efficiency by reinforcing desirable performances and eliminating the unacceptable ones.

How to Calculate Your Target

Start by preparing a recipe sheet for every item on the menu. Here the chef will break down the item to its ingredients in ounces. He or she will determine how much is needed to produce the item on the menu, taking into consideration the yield, defined as the usable portion from each ingredient after the normal peeling, trimming, ageing, shrinking, waste, etc. In other words the chef will be concerned with the quantity of each ingredient as purchased, not as served.

Cost all recipes based on current ingredient prices adjusted to reflect the normal and expected fluctuations for the coming 12 months or for the duration of the menu. Determine the sale price for every item on the menu, taking into consideration not only the cost of the food but also the elasticity of the demand, the type and quality of service, other operating expenses, and—above all—the competition.

There are two different ways to calculate what the food cost should be (food cost potential):

A.) 1. Add the cost of all items to produce the menu's total cost.

2. Add the sale price for all items to produce the menu's total sales.

3. Based on the assumption that sales will be equal amongst all the items, divide menu total cost (from A-1) by menu total sales (from A-2). The result is your food cost potential.

B.) 1. Assume a certain sales mix based on past experience and/or certain expectations.

2. Figure out the total sales for that sales mix.

3. Figure out the total cost for that sales mix.

4. Divide the total cost dollars by the total sales dollars and the result is your food cost potential.

Approach A is more acceptable in a computerised environment, assuming that the cost for every item as per the recipe sheet will be entered in the system and kept up to date. Only then can the customer preference report be meaningful. Regardless of how you are going to calculate it, the food cost potential should be realistic and attainable or the whole exercise will be meaningless.

Just remember that if the food operation happens to have more than one outlet or more than one menu, you need to calculate a separate food cost potential for every menu and an average for the whole food operation.

Performance Analysing

The amount of time and effort required to do the monthly food cost analysis will depend mainly on the type of information (system and equipment) available and the experience of the people involved. The following are the steps to be taken to analyse the performance in the food cost area.

1. Ensure that the targeted food cost percentage for the period is more than just wishful thinking. The target must be the calculated food cost potential.

2. Check the accuracy of your records. It is quite possible that the alarming food cost percentage is nothing more than a clerical error in accounting factors such as the value of the inventory or the accruals.
3. Prepare a comprehensive and precise list of all the factors (reasons) that can affect the food cost percentage in your operation.
4. Determine which of these factors affected the food cost percentage during the period.
5. Quantify (measure) the effect of each factor on the total food cost in dollar terms or percentage.
6. List these factors in groups that can make your analysis more meaningful, and easier to read and prepare.
7. Prepare your monthly report and write your comments, including the type of corrective actions to be taken to improve performance.

For your food cost analysis to be more meaningful, productive, and useful to your operation, the main factors that affect the food cost percentage must be identified. They can be classified into the following three groups namely the accounting factors, the controllable factors, and the uncontrollable factors.

Accounting Factors

The purpose of this classification is to list the exact areas where you should audit to ensure the accuracy of your records as far as food cost is concerned. Remember that food cost analysis based on inaccurate records is not only a waste of time but can also be damaging if decisions are made based on such misleading results. Any undetected error in the following areas is considered a factor that will distort food cost results and create unexplained variances. Accordingly, every area should be audited, making corrections if needed and confirming that the records in each area are accurate.

Mixing up billings between periods: The cutoff date between accounting periods is very important. Processing a food invoice in January that was actually purchased and delivered in February will produce an inaccurate food cost percentage for both January and February.

Over-billing: Undetected errors on the supplier's invoice, such as the wrong quantity, unit, price per unit, or an arithmetic error would affect your food cost analysis. For example, receiving two jars of apple sauce and processing an invoice for two cases of apple sauce will obviously inflate the cost of food if not caught and corrected.

Coding error: Any wrong posting to the food cost account will affect your analysis. It is possible that the light bulb invoice was coded by accident as food or the beer bottle refund was credited to food cost, etc.

Inventory inaccuracy: Inaccuracy of the closing or the opening inventory will affect the food cost result for the period. The inaccuracy could be in the inventory count, the unit, the price per unit, and/or the extension.

Transactions from and to food: Inaccurate transactions between the food as a profit center and other profit centers could affect the food cost results—for example, transactions such as food to bar, beverages for cooking, food for mix, office usage, house promotion, etc.

Accruals inaccuracy: Error in food accruals for current or last period, defined as the cost of food that was ordered and received but the invoice has not been processed, will affect food cost results.

Accounting treatment inconsistency: Inconsistency in the accounting treatment from one period to another will have an effect on food cost. For example, the accounting treatment for a food delivery charge, the cost of staff meals, or the method of pricing the inventory must be consistent from one period to another or food cost results will reflect such variances.

House use unaccounted for: There is always the possibility that ingredients or prepared food was legitimately issued to or used by the house but no record was made or kept as a result of a weak internal control. Such unaccounted for house use, regardless of the intention, will affect the food cost.

Giveaways not recorded: Giveaways such as fruit baskets or any complimentary food item issued to a guest or potential guest which was not recorded or accounted for will have an effect on the food cost results if not caught and corrected during the period.

Short deliveries and returned items: Regardless of the intention, there is always the possibility that food items are ordered and paid for, yet never received. Also there is a possibility that certain items were rejected and returned to the supplier and no record was made or kept because of weak internal control. Food cost will be inflated by these mix-ups.

Inaccurate sales records: Regardless of the intention, food sales understated, and/or overstated will have an impact on the food cost percentage.

Controllable Factors

The purpose of this classification is to highlight at a glance who is responsible for what and what kind of action is needed to rectify the situation. The term controllable vs. uncontrollable is a relative one. In other words, from the responsibility point of view, the factors that we might consider uncontrollable at the chef's level where the responsibility for food costs lies, could be controllable at the general manager's level. The following factors are considered controllable from the point of view of the total operation.

A cut in menu prices (discounts): If the sales or service personnel cut the menu prices, the food cost percentage will be affected. To measure the effect of cutting prices, reconstruct the sales figures assuming that the discount did not take place, calculate a new food cost percentage, then subtract it from the actual food cost percentage. The difference is the effect of cutting the prices on the food cost percentage.

Changing the recipe (portion size/ingredients quality): In the production area (the kitchen), deviating from the standard recipe will affect the food cost. For example, using larger portions or more expensive ingredients will produce a higher food cost, whereas reducing the portion or using cheaper ingredients will have the opposite impact on food cost, but quite possibly a negative impact on food sales, especially in the long run. It is not easy to measure the effect of this factor on the food cost. However, an experienced chef will be able to figure out the effect in dollars.

Lower quality ingredients could also mean more waste during production (in trimming, peeling, shrinking, etc.) or in rejected meals by the customer. Measuring the effect of this factor on food cost requires some creativity.

Buy vs. make: A change in management philosophy from making certain items in-house to buying them from outside, or a change towards buying more processed items might have a positive effect on labor costs, but will definitely have a negative effect on the food cost. To quantify the effect of such a factor, use your spreadsheet and subtract the cost of buying from the cost of making (as per recipe) for the quantity purchased during the period.

Damage, spoilage, and waste: Damage or waste caused by a layout problem, unclean and/or disorganised storage, and new or poorly trained staff, regardless of whether it is in the receiving, storage, production, or service areas, will affect food cost. The effect of this factor should be identified, measured, and reported separately. To measure the effect of this factor on food cost, first ensure that all damage, spoilage, and waste are reported in detail. The damage report should list the item name, description, units, quantity, and most importantly, what caused the damage. Then cost and group the reports based on the cause of the damage and total them for the period.

Order size: Quantity discounts sometimes lures the buyer to increase the size of his order. In this case the effect on food cost should be positive. However we cannot ignore the cost of financing the excess inventory, the possibility of more damage and spoilage in a crowded storage, and that some ingredients will not be as fresh as they should be. On the other hand, if the buyer places an order smaller than the agreed on minimum, the price could be higher and the effect on the food cost will be negative. The effect of this factor on food cost should be identified, calculated and reported separately. To measure the effect of this factor in dollar terms, analyse the change in prices for every order that was over the maximum or under the minimum during the period.

Equipment malfunction: Equipment malfunction can have an effect on food cost. For example, a freezer breakdown can damage hundreds of dollars worth of meat or ice cream. The effect of such a factor on food cost should be identified, totalled, and reported separately.

Theft and sabotage: If theft takes place in the establishment, a higher food cost will be unavoidable. Also staff anger and hostile attitudes toward management can create unnecessary damage and waste. Obviously measuring the effect of this factor on food cost is not an easy one. One way to put a dollar value on this factor is to rely on the chef's close supervision, taking inventory more often and between shifts, checking the garbage bins before dumping, documenting, and reporting the cost of missing items.

Other controllable factors: Any controllable factors that may not fall into the above areas belong in this category. A poorly designed menu might confuse customers, who may reject the cooked items. The effect of a late order (orders needed yesterday) may create unnecessary expense. Take for example, a $ 25 taxi receipt to deliver a $ 5 food item that was not ordered on time. This is an expense that should have been avoided. The effect of all these factors should be calculated and reported separately.

Uncontrollable Factors

Some factors in the food operation cannot be foreseen during the planning stage. However, they can still have an effect on the food cost and must be taken into consideration when analysing performance in the food cost area.

Sales mix: Because some items on the menu cost more to produce than others, customers' choices will affect the food cost results. For example, producing breakfast items normally costs less than producing dinner items. Accordingly, more dinner sales than breakfast sales would mean a higher food cost and vice versa. The operation will calculate its food cost potential based on a certain food sales mix and nothing can be done if the customer's choice produces a different sales mix.

The impact of such an uncontrollable factor on food cost could be substantial. In your analysis you should be able to identify and account for the effect of this factor on total food cost. It is much easier to measure that effect when you have a computerised system in the food and beverage area. All you have to do is subtract the actual food cost percentage from the food cost potential, weighted by the actual sales mix which is one figure on the customer's preference report. The only way to avoid the impact of the sales mix on food cost is to price all items at the same cost percentage. Unfortunately this approach is not practical.

Unpredictable climate: This factor looks at the effect of unforeseen weather that can affect produce prices. For example, a cold snap in the South, an unusually hot, dry summer in the North, or a rainy spring out West affects produce prices. This should be identified, calculated, and reported separately. To quantify the effect of this factor, list the main food items on a typical spreadsheet and subtract the price of each item as planned in the recipe from the price paid during the period. Then multiply the difference by the quantity purchased during the period.

Other uncontrollable factors. Factors to be considered include new taxes, tariffs, embargoes and regulations, labor strikes by the main food suppliers, etc.

Food Cost Analysis Report

Finally, you are now ready to present your notes, calculations, estimates, judgments, measurements, evaluation, opinions, and the results of your analysis by preparing the food cost analysis report. One person should be responsible for preparing the monthly food cost analysis report, usually the food and beverage controller. It is also important to emphasize that a good food cost analysis will not be possible without the participation of the chef and the food and beverage manager.

The food cost analysis report shown is designed for a simple food operation with one kitchen. It highlights the type of data collected and how to present it. If you have more than one kitchen, a large food operation, or your needs are slightly different, then tailor your report accordingly.

The report indicates that the actual food cost percentage for the period as per the financial statements was better than the budgeted one. It also proves that relying on just this statement could be misleading. As the report clearly indicates, the actual food cost percentage should have been even better. Examine the report to identify the results of inefficiency in certain areas, which offset the results of the good performance in other areas.

The report shows that only a food cost analysis will properly evaluate the performances in the food cost area and produce more meaningful findings. It should be discussed and approved by the financial controller before distribution.

Rising Food Prices

Income growth, climate change, high energy prices, globalisation, and urbanisation are all converging to transform food production, markets, and consumption, according to a new report by the International Food Policy Research Institute (IFPRI). As a result, global food demand and prices are likely to rise, threatening the livelihoods and nutrition of poor people in developing countries. The report, "The World Food Situation: New Driving Forces and Required Actions," was released today at the annual general meeting of the Consultative Group on International Agricultural Research (CGIAR).

"Food prices have been steadily decreasing since the Green Revolution, but the days of falling food prices may be over," said Joachim von Braun, lead author of the report and director general of IFPRI. "Surging demand for feed, food, and fuel have recently led to drastic price increases, which are not likely to fall in the foreseeable future, due to low stocks and slow-growing supplies of agricultural outputs. Climate change will also have a negative impact on food production, compounding the challenge of meeting global food demand, and potentially exacerbating hunger and malnutrition among the world's poorest people."

"Economic growth has helped to reduce hunger, particularly when it is equitable," added von Braun. "But unfortunately, growth does not always reach the poorest people."

Consumer Demand

Many regions of the developing world, especially China and India, have seen high economic growth in recent years. Together with an expanding urban population, income growth is altering spending and consumer preferences. Global food demand is shifting from grains and other staple crops to processed food and high-value agricultural products, such as vegetables, fruits, meat, and dairy. Although many smallholder farmers would like to take advantage of new income-generating opportunities presented by high-value products, there are serious barriers to entering this market, including the capacity to address safety and quality standards and produce large quantities for food processors and retailers.

Bioenergy

In response to rising oil costs, the production of biofuels as an alternative source of energy is also contributing to dramatic changes in the world food situation. According to the report, increased production of bioenergy will adversely affect poor people in developing countries by increasing both the price and price volatility of food.

Subsidies for biofuels, which are common, exacerbate the negative impact on poor households, as they implicitly act as a tax on basic food.

Using state-of-the-art computer modeling, IFPRI has projected the possible price effects of biofuels for two potential scenarios up to the year 2020:

— Under scenario one, which is based on the actual biofuel investment plans of many countries and the assumption that high-potential countries will expand their production of bioenergy, maize prices would increase by 26 percent and oilseed prices would rise by 18 percent.

— Under scenario two, which assumes that the production of biofuels would expand greatly, to twice the level of scenario one, maize prices would increase by 72 percent and oilseeds by 44 percent.

In both scenarios, rises in crop prices would lead to decreases in food availability and calorie consumption in all regions of the world, with Sub-Saharan Africa suffering the most. As biofuels become increasingly profitable, more land, water, and capital will be diverted to their production, and the world will face more trade-offs between food and fuel.

Agricultural Trade

China and almost all African countries, which are net importers of cereals, would suffer from the resulting high prices, but India, a net exporter would benefit. Overall, the majority of poor people, who live in households that are net buyers of food, will be worse off and increased food prices will make it even more difficult for them to eat healthy, well-balanced diets.

A more open global trade in agriculture, however, would generally benefit developing countries. IFPRI research shows that opening up and facilitating market access between industrialised and developing countries would bring significant economic gains, although poverty would not be significantly reduced except in certain contexts.

Climate Change

World agricultural output is projected to decrease significantly due to global warming, and the impact on developing countries will be much more severe than on industrialised nations. Africa is particularly vulnerable to climate change because of its high proportion of low-input, rainfed agriculture, compared with Asia or Latin America. Exposure to rainfall variability also extends to livestock, which mostly depend on range and grasslands that are affected by environmental shocks, such as climate change. To address these risks, investments to improve agricultural productivity need to increase and innovative insurance mechanisms should be explored to compensate rural communities and smallholder farmers when rains fail.

Policy Recommendations

Given the various risks and challenges posed by the rapidly changing world food situation, current market trends and government policies could exacerbate hunger and poverty, especially for the world's poorest people. Policymakers thus must take explicit measures to mitigate the negatives effects on poor households. While tackling long-term challenges is vital, the report recommends that policymakers also take immediate action:

Developed countries should facilitate flexible responses to drastic changes in food prices by eliminating trade barriers and programs that set aside agriculture resources. A world facing increased food scarcity needs to trade more, not less.

Developing countries should increase investment in rural infrastructure and market institutions to improve access to critical agricultural inputs, including fertilisers, seeds, and credit, which are key to enhancing productivity. To counteract rising food prices, national and international research systems, including the CGIAR, should be positioned to invest more heavily in agricultural science and technology to increase agricultural production on a global level.

Policymakers should enact social protection measures that focus on early childhood nutrition to mitigate risks associated with reduced food access, particularly for the poorest households. Because poor people in developing countries are especially vulnerable to the risks associated with climate change, particularly as it relates to food security, policymakers should take agriculture and food issues into account when developing national and international climate change agendas.

Branding and Repositioning Food & Beverage

Hotel guests generally enjoy the convenience of F&B outlets, hut when given the chance, they frequently choose a known brand off the premises, leaving a hotel for nearby restaurant chains. In the process, they take much-desired dining dollars with them. As customers become more brand-aware, competition for F&B business continues to grow in importance for many hotels. From the hotel's perspective, a joint venture or outsourcing arrangement can provide a combination of restaurant skills and brand strength, often supported by national advertising. Hotels adding branded restaurants have reported improved F&B volume, including room service sales, as well as an attendant increase in occupancy and average rate. In a period of hospitality industry consolidation, branded restaurants may become a point of differentiation among hotel properties.

Restaurant companies, of course, also stand to gain from this flurry of alliances. In today's market, many companies are being forced to look outside traditional development options and to consider new types of locations. Given these benefits, it is surprising there is not more outsourcing of food and beverage in the hotel industry.

Competencies and Outsourcing

During the early 1990s, businesses faced the difficult task of assessing procedural strengths and weaknesses to trim fat and streamline processes. Outsourcing non-critical activities allowed companies to extend their organisational core competencies. The hospitality and leisure industry was no exception to this trend. During the past few years, hotels have been called on to assess their core competencies, while attempting to shed responsibility for non-core activities.

Core competencies can be defined as those unique disciplines that confer competitive advantage, motivating customers to buy a company's goods and services over those of a competitor. As this decade comes to a close, businesses are further dividing the non-core segment into two categories: "essential non-core" and "non-essential non-core." Those activities that are both non-core and non-essential are being shut down. Processes that are essential, but "non-core," become prime candidates for outsourcing. Providing quality rooms and guest services remains a hotel's primary function.

The F&B function, however, commands attention because of its importance to guest satisfaction and brand management. Many hoteliers, however, make the mistake of thinking that it takes the same competencies to operate a restaurant as it does to run a hotel. In actual fact, the restaurant business requires a different set of skills, including more attention to detail, than rooms management. By reengineering F&B operations, hotel management has the opportunity to redirect energies from the restaurant business and focus efforts on enhancing hotel operations and profitability and, potentially, shareholder value. This raises important questions for management.

Outsourcing Equation

Outsourcing partnerships typically bring together organisations with diverse capabilities. Understanding what each side of the equation requires to succeed is essential. This important guideline applies whether a hotel owner is considering outsourcing all or part of its F&B operations to a restaurant chain, or merely outsourcing its coffee shop to a local restaurateur.

Historically, restaurant chains have been strict about the demographics and economic indicators in a market before committing to a location. And until recently, there was no shortage of suitable sites. Prime demographic indicators include a mix of office space, upper-middle class residences, and upscale apartments with higher-income professionals looking for an element of fun. If a potential restaurant site was not viewed as a "home run" location, a restaurateur would typically pass on a development opportunity. Due to increased competition and a limited number of prime sites, restaurant companies have found they must go further afield than in the past, breaking traditional biases about what locations work.

Until recently, hotels have been reluctant to outsource their F&B operations - or single restaurants. Traditionally, hotel management viewed F&B operations as a low margin or unprofitable service required to enhance guest satisfaction. As such, F&B profitability was always examined with a mentality of "minimising a loss." As a way to rationalise an unprofitable track record, hotel management often convinced itself that there was insufficient demand for profitable F&B operations. In addition, as hotels emerged from the last recession and downturn in hotel profitability, emphasis was placed on the renovation of guestrooms, lobbies and banquet space over F&B outlets. Based on historical trends, renovation priority has consistently been given to profit-generating guestrooms over unprofitable food and beverage operations.

Additionally, hotels opting to create a new concept or introduce an existing, branded concept may find start-up costs to he exorbitant. Estimated costs of upgrading a food and beverage outlet to a chain's specified standards range from $500,000 to $1.5 million, depending on the extent of renovation and equipment purchases required. Of course, outsourcing operations to a local restaurateur would likely cost far less. The hotel, however, would not benefit from the brand recognition associated with a larger, more established name in the marketplace.

Lastly, hotel management companies earning fees based on gross revenue may be reluctant to reduce the base on which their management fee is calculated. This may prompt hotel owners and managers to reassess their management position. Frequently the parties agree to either renegotiate revenue-based fee percentages or include revenues earned by third-party F&B operators in the management fee calculations.

Despite the issues associated with outsourcing of food and beverage operations, there are compelling reasons for hotels to consider this option. Brand strength and competitive positioning for the hotel property are among the most important.

Branding and Repositioning

While consumers are more brand aware than ever before, research suggests there may even be a perceived stigma associated with dining in a hotel restaurant. Integrating a branded concept into a hotel is a way to minimise the stigma, bringing guests back to the hotel outlets and reducing internal costs. Additionally, familiar dining concepts seem to put travelers at ease. Customers who are away from home and out of their element are comforted by the availability and consistency that accompanies a known brand name product.

In addition to brand identity, most operators find that guests are not only more willing to patronise high-street brands conveniently situated within the hotel, but they are also willing to pay more for the privilege of dining with a familiar concept. Increased willingness to dine coupled with increased willingness to spend results in increased revenues.

Hotels introducing a branded restaurant into their property often experience higher external traffic. Market exposure translates into increased outlet revenue and enhanced customer perception of the F&B outlet brand name, as well as enhanced customer perception of the hotel itself. Thus the net result of rebranding and repositioning can be increased profit and enhanced shareholder value.

Before taking the plunge into the world of outsourced or reengineered F&B operations, hotel management must take several factors into consideration:

Competition: No outsourcing arrangement will work, unless there is market demand. Competitive analysis should include restaurants in neighboring hotels, as well as stand-alone restaurants in the area. Profitability issues and pricing a new outlet also must be considered in the market context. Many hotels find that the brand name restaurant buys recognition in the customer 5 mind and creates a draw for business. The partnered restaurant sets the hotel apart from other hotels in the area and segment by providing a strong competitive and marketing advantage.

Marketing: The hotelier and restaurateur must establish responsibility for marketing of the new concept. Frequently hotels agree to advertise the operator in the guestrooms, although the outlet typically absorbs the cost of signage in the rooms and throughout the hotel. Additionally, the restaurateur typically assumes responsibility and accountability for all external advertising.

Guest expectations: The goal of outsourcing F&B operations is to enhance profitability by increasing internal as well as external traffic, without losing the current customer base. It is essential to consider guest reaction to the change in F&B concept. If a negative reaction is anticipated, a hotelier risks losing its customer base and thus future earning potential to the competition.

Management styles: It is important to look at both the local and corporate management styles of both the hotelier and restaurateur, Incompatibility of the two styles could result in a rocky relationship and tumultuous times. In order to avoid this friction, some hotels have found it advantageous to appoint the general manager of the restaurant to the hotel's executive team, thereby creating a sense of responsibility and belonging and enhancing relationships throughout the organisation.

Terms of the Contract: The operational terms of the contract must be set out in detail. Quality standards and monitoring mechanisms should be detailed to ensure that the restaurant is operated at a standard that is acceptable and complementary to that of the hotel. Additionally, hours of restaurant operation, including room service, are critical specifications. As breakfast is typically a money - generating activity, and frequently not one that restaurant chain operators are accustomed to serving, many hoteliers prefer to maintain responsibility for this meal. However, concessions affecting profitability occasionally need to be made in order to solidify a working relationship.

A successful outsourcing relationship involves first and foremost trust and cohesion between the two partners. Of course, operational terms must be clearly detailed and make economic sense for both parties. While the requirements of a restaurant chain may be more stringent and costly than those of an independent restaurant operator, the basic tenets of a trusting partnership, complementary levels of quality, compatible clientele and a location with sufficient demand to justify a restaurant operation are all necessary. Successful implementation of an F&B outsourcing partnership can result in enhanced brand recognition and profitability for both the hotelier and the restaurateur.

Structuring an Outsourcing Partnership

Leasing: A hotel leases a room or section of the hotel, preferably with self-contained back-of-the-house areas in exchange for a flat fee and/or a percentage of sales. Statistics are not available for this type of transaction, as leasing deals vary depending on the area of space being leased, the brand being introduced into the market, the location of the hotel and agreements that may have been established by a head office. The hotel benefits by receiving a guaranteed rent, plus a revenue "top-up" each month. The landlord, however, loses control of F&B operations. Management must agree to let someone else run the show.

Franchising: This option suits a hotel seeking to change a restaurant concept without investing in an internal and potentially untested concept. The hotel buys an established brand and system for a fee. The process begins with an upfront payment - a buy-in to the right to operate a better known and more profitable concept. Frequently, the franchisor requires the hotel to make an additional payment for a capital investment, requiring a purchase of specified equipment. Under the franchising terms, the hotel pays the franchisor a royalty fee, usually based on a percentage of sales, for the privilege of using the name and resources.

Throughout the relationship, it is the franchisees responsibility to ensure that hotel staff is adequately trained to assure quality consistent with other branded sites. Marriott International was one of the first major hotel chains to enter into F&B franchising arrangements, with a 1989 franchising partnership with Pizza Hut. Marriott has since introduced Pizza Hut outlets and in-room dining options at many of its properties throughout the world.

Joint Venture: This is a variant of franchising and contracting. The hotelier creates a strategic alliance with a known, successful restaurateur. The two parties create a separate financial company, which is appointed as the lessee of the restaurant. The new organisation, the restaurant lessee., then outsources the F&B operations to the restaurateur. Typically the hotel provides the capital expenditures and the restaurateur brings intellectual property and expertise. The two parties share the successes and the related profits.

Proprietary Brands: Hotel chains can create a proprietary brand, introducing the concept into all of its properties. This approach appeals to guests who enjoy consistency throughout a hotel chain. However, it is difficult to gain wider customer identity outside of the hotel properties.

9

Standard Purchase Specification

The menu determines products that must be purchased. If items are not needed, they should not be purchased. While this seems obvious, the rusty, dusty cans in some storerooms and the pounds of frozen products stored for a year or more in freezers suggest that this principle is not always followed. Likewise, in beverage operations, purchasing needs are determined by the menu. Many managers feel they must offer an extremely large selection of various call brand products, which may spend most of their time on the shelf. A better approach may be to offer a limited range of popular call brands while keeping other call brands on hand for regular guests.

While the menu's impact on the control system is obvious, cost control also depends on the skills and abilities of purchasing personnel and others who work within the food and beverage operation. If ineffective management and staff personnel are employed, no amount of planning and control can ensure success.

Since cost savings in food and beverage purchasing go directly to the bottom line, no hospitality operation can afford inefficient purchasing procedures. Consider the following example. Let's assume that the profits earned by a food and beverage operation are eight percent of the revenue generated. This means that for every dollar of revenue, the operation earns a profit of eight cents. Let's assume that poor purchasing practices waste $500 every week. How much must the operation generate in additional revenue to pay for the wasted $500? The answer is not $500 dollars. Revenue must also be used to pay for food costs, beverage costs, necessary labour costs, mortgage payments, taxes, and many other types of costs as well. The wasted $500 must come out of the operation's profits.

So, to maintain an eight percent profit level, the operation must earn the $500 lost in profit by generating additional weekly revenue of $6,250. No operation can afford to allocate its first $6,250 in revenue each week to offset higher-than-necessary costs which could have been reduced by effective purchasing. Although the control process is affected by decisions made in all areas of the complex food and beverage management system, it is convenient to begin discussing food and beverage cost control where the physical cycle of the operation begins-at the purchasing and receiving control points. However, actual cost control begins when goals for purchasing and receiving are established. Many plans and procedures are already in place before the physical cycle begins.

Purchasing Objectives and Procedures

Purchasing is the series of activities designed to obtain products of the right quality and quantity, at the right price and time, and from the right source. These simple objectives can be difficult to achieve. Since the purchasing cycle involves a variety of different procedures, many activities must be controlled when designing and managing purchasing tasks. The purchasing cycle involves the following activities:

— The chef in the food department and the bartender (or bar manager) in the beverage department complete an issue requisition when items are needed.

— The storeroom responds by issuing required products to the user department.

— When products in inventory reach a predetermined reorder point, the storeroom forwards a purchase requisition to the purchasing department.

— The purchasing department orders required products from the proper supplier, perhaps using a purchase order or a purchase record. Increasingly, food service operators place orders with suppliers using e-commerce (business-to business) technology. Purchasing personnel send or transmit the purchase order or purchase record information to the receiving and accounting departments.

— The supplier delivers the products to the receiving department along with a delivery invoice.

— The receiving clerk places products in the storeroom and forwards the delivery invoice, perhaps with other documents, to the accounting department. In some properties, these forms are reviewed by the food and beverage management staff before being routed to accounting personnel.

— After further processing of necessary documents, accounting department personnel send payment to the supplier and file copies of the purchasing/receiving forms for accounting and/ or control purposes.

This purchasing cycle is repeated every time products are ordered. You can see that purchasing is more than II picking up the phone and calling in an order." It is a complex cycle of activities requiring special planning and control procedures that create an audit trail. An audit trail is a series of records, documents, and/ or reports that trace the flow of resources through an operation.

Responsibility for Purchasing

Ultimate responsibility for purchasing decisions generally lies with the food and beverage manager. In small operations, the general manager may function as a food and beverage manager. In very small properties, the owner, manager, and food and beverage manager are frequently the same individual. As properties increase in size, positions become more specialised.

In a small hotel, for example, the food and beverage manager (who may perform many duties frequently done by individuals in different positions in larger properties) may be responsible for purchasing. In large food and beverage operations, a staff purchasing agent may be assigned to perform the many activities that may be necessary. When a purchasing agent is employed, it is important to recall the difference between a line position and staff position. As the name suggests, line managers are in the chain of command. They make the decisions affecting the food and beverage operation. Examples of line positions include the general manager, food and beverage manager, lower-level supervisors, and entry-level employees. By contrast, staff personnel provide specialised technical and advisory assistance to line managers.

The purchasing agent, therefore, is in a staff (advisory) relationship to the food and beverage manager. As such, purchasing agents should not make decisions involving, for example, the definition of required quality, whether items should be purchased in convenience form or be prepared on-site, or whether purchase quantities should be increased or decreased to reflect price trends. These and numerous other decision-making tasks applicable to purchasing should be done by line personnel with suggestions from staff purchasing officials. In this regard, the purchasing agent functions in much the same way as does a personnel officer, accountant, or public relations official; the purchasing agent studies problems and gives advice but does not make purchasing decisions. Generally, it is the food and beverage manager who bears ultimate responsibility for purchasing decisions.

Selecting Suppliers

Managers of food and beverage operations should choose suppliers carefully. Detailed purchase specifications and objective calculations of quantities to order are ineffective without professional suppliers. Essentially, the food and beverage manager bases supplier evaluations on the consistency of:

— Correct quality products

— Reasonable prices

— Prompt delivery

— Service, including product information

When selecting suppliers, the purchasers must consider a number of factors. Not every supplier who carries the needed product is appropriate for the food and beverage operation. The supplier with the lowest price may not be "right" for the operation, either. The following are important factors to consider when selecting a supplier.

— *Location.* Delivery time, transportation costs, and unexpected delays may be reduced if the supplier's facility is close to the food and beverage operation.

— *Quality of the Supplier's Operation.* Such things as sanitation, inhouse processing, handling of orders, and the quantity and quality of items in stock must be assessed. Technical Ability of the Supplier's Staff. Good salespersons are more than order-takers. They know their products and can help the operation resolve problems involving the products they supply.

— *Value.* The purchaser must carefully assess the supplier's prices in relation to the quality of products needed by the operation. Compatibility. A good working relationship between the food and beverage purchaser and the supplier requires mutual beliefs about ethics and the fair treatment of both the guests and the supplier.

— *Honesty and Fairness.* These traits must be part of the ongoing business relationship and the supplier's reputation. Delivery Personnel. Their appearance, attitude, and courtesy contribute to the impression formed by the food and beverage operation.

The purchasing manager should identify all possible sources for all items needed, determine the best suppliers, and choose from among them. While longstanding relationships with suppliers can help in future dealings, managers should be careful not to get too comfortable with their suppliers. There is the danger of allowing standards to slip so that the property is not getting the most from its purchasing dollar. Therefore, it is appropriate to periodically review the selection of suppliers and assess their performance in meeting the operation's expectations.

Purchasing the Proper Quality

In relation to the purchasing function, the term quality refers to the suitability of a product for its intended use. The more suitable a product, the higher its quality. For example, a super colossal olive may represent the right quality product for garnish or salad purposes. It may not, however, represent the proper quality if it is to be chopped and used as a salad bar topping. Decisions about quality requirements are first made when the goals of the business are established and subsequent marketing plans are developed. At that time, the spirit and intent of the food and beverage operation's quality standards are determined. Later, standard purchase specifications are documented in detail to indicate the requirements for products suitable for every intended purpose. These specifications provide detailed descriptions of the quality, size, and weight desired for particular items.

The relationship between quality and price is referred to as value. Just as the guest considers value when deciding what to order the restaurant or lounge, food and beverage managers must also consider value when choosing products to purchase. To purchase products of optimal value for the food and beverage operation, the purchaser must carefully evaluate each product's quality (suitability for intended use) in relation to its cost. Notice that it not only describes the desired product, but also specifies how the product will be used. In addition, it informs the supplier about the operation's procedures for ensuring that the delivered item does, in fact, meet the required quality specifications. Standard purchase specifications must:

— Accurately describe minimum quality requirements
— Clearly and simply indicate the food and beverage operation's needs
— Realistically define needs, yet not limit the number of acceptable suppliers

Generally, specifications should be developed for all products purchased. However, there is a need to be practical in following this principle. Developing detailed specifications for products such as salt and other seasonings or bar swizzle sticks is often not justified. Instead, managers involved with the purchasing function should first develop specifications for expensive, highvolume items and then formalize quality requirements for other products as time permits.

When items are purchased by brand, such as liquor or ketchup, the brand itself becomes the specification.

However, it is still necessary to specify container size and special instructions. Another purchasing tool is the food sample data sheet. This sheet helps standardise the evaluation of a product. It can be used to record purchasing, storing, preparing, and serving information about products that the operation is sampling and considering for purchase. The food sample data sheet makes product selection more objective.

Purchasing the Sufficient Quantities

Purchasing the proper quantities of items is just as important as developing correct quality specifications. Problems that can arise when too much of a product is ordered include:

- — Cash flow problems resulting from excessive money tied up in inventory
- — Increased storage costs such as interest, insurance, and, sometimes, rented storage space
- — Deterioration in quality, or damaged products
- — Increased chance of theft and pilferage

Purchasing insufficient quantities also has potential disadvantages such as dissatisfied guests due to stockouts, emergency and rush orders which are frequently expensive and timeconsuming, and lost discounts from volume purchases. To avoid these problems, food and beverage managers must periodically assess a number of factors that affect the purchase of proper quantities. These factors include the following:

- — *Popularity of Menu Items.* As unit sales of menu items increase, additional quantities of ingredients are obviously needed.
- — *Product Cost Concerns.* Higher product costs may result in increased selling prices, which, in turn, may result in decreased sales levels. In this case, the need for

continued purchase of the product should be evaluated. Also, management may make judgments about future prices and buy more if prices are expected to increase or less if prices are expected to decrease. This is called speculative purchasing and should only be done by management based upon information provided by the purchaser.

— *Available Storage Space.* Available space may limit quantities purchased. Storage space in dry, frozen, and refrigerated areas may not be adequate to accommodate quantity purchases. Safety Level. Maintaining a safety level of products in inventory may require buying a quantity above that actually needed to allow for delivery delays, increased usage, or other unexpected developments.

— *Supplier Constraints.* For example, suppliers may specify minimum dollar and/ or poundage requirements for delivery. Also, some suppliers may not break cases, bags, or other packing containers to meet overly specific order quantities. Therefore, the standard commercial units of the packaging influence quantities purchased.

Perishable Products

Perishable items (such as fresh produce, bakery, and dairy products) should be used as soon as possible. These types of products are normally purchased several times weekly according to the following formula:

Quantity Needed - Quantity Available = Quantity to Purchase for Immediate Use

Sample procedures for purchasing perishable products are as follows:

— Determine normal usage rates. For example, assess, for a normal two-day purchasing period, the specific number of cases of selected produce items, pounds of fresh meat, fresh poultry fryers, and other perishable products the property typically uses.

— Assess the amount of each item currently in inventory.

— Calculate the quantity to purchase by subtracting the quantity available from the quantity needed.

— Adjust routine quantities as necessary for special functions, holidays, or other unique circumstances.

Non-Perishable Products

To determine the quantity of non-perishable products to purchase, it is often practical to use a minimum/ maximum system of inventory management. This system is based upon the concept of " A" items discussed earlier; only a few of all items purchased represent high-cost or high-frequency items. Minimum/ maximum ordering systems give first attention to these high-priority items and help managers determine when products must be purchased and how much of each product to order.

For each purchase item, the minimum/maximum ordering system assesses the minimum quantity below which inventory levels should not fall and the maximum quantity above which inventory levels should not rise. The minimum inventory level is the safety level-the number of purchase units that must always remain in inventory. The maximum inventory level is the greatest number of purchase units permitted in storage. The maximum inventory level of purchase units permitted in storage is the usage rate plus the minimum (safety) level. The most important factor for determining when more purchase units must be ordered is, of course, the rate at which they are used by the operation.

The usage rate is the number of purchase units used per order period. Purchase units are counted in terms of the number of shipping containers of normal size for each product. For example, if ten cases (six number-10 cans) of green peas are normally used between deliveries, the usage rate for green peas is ten cases. In addition to usage rates, managers must determine a leadtime quantity for each purchase item.

The leadtime quantity is the number of purchase units withdrawn from inventory between the time an order is placed and when it is delivered. Again, purchase units are counted in terms of normal size shipping containers. For example, if two cases of green peas are used between ordering and receiving, the leadtime quantity is two cases. This leadtime quantity is separate from the safety (minimum) level of purchase units kept in inventory. The safety level must allow for such things as late deliveries and greater than normal usage.

The order point is the number of purchase units in stock when an order is placed. The order point is reached when the number of purchase units in inventory equals the leadtime quantity plus the safety level:

Purchase Units at	=	Purchase Unit in	+	Purchase Unit in
Order Point		Lead Time		Safety level

If products are ordered at the order point, the quantity in inventory will be reduced to the safety (minimum) level by the time products are received. When the order arrives, the inventory level for the product will again be brought back to the maximum level.

Purchase Order System

So far, the control procedures that apply prior to the actual purchasing task. Before the purchasing process begins, the food and beverage operation should have specified minimum quality standards, calculated quantities of products to be purchased, determined order points for each purchase item, and considered eligible suppliers. It is important that control procedures be built into the actual purchasing process as well. For this purpose, large food and beverage operations use a purchase order system.

With a purchase order system, a purchase order is sent (by mail, fax, or email) to the supplier awarded the order. Information about the order is retained in the purchasing department and is also circulated internally among the receiving and accounting departments. The purchase order formally identifies the product, quantity, unit cost, and total cost that both the supplier and purchaser have agreed upon. In addition, the purchase order may include guarantees, warranties, payment requirements, inspection rights, "hold harmless" provisions, and other legal, contractual concerns.

The property must pay the agreedupon price for no less than the agreedupon quality for the amount ordered. Higher than necessary food and beverage costs are frequently traced to communication and coordination problems among the several departments or personnel involved in purchasing. Property used, the purchase order minimizes these problems.

Rather than using a purchase order system, smaller food and beverage operations may simply summarize purchase order information by using an inhouse purchase record form. The purchase record performs the same functions as the purchase order. It provides the food and beverage operation with a detailed record of all incoming shipments. Affected personnel and departments must know all the specifics about incoming food and beverage products. Without a written record, busy management staff may forget the details. Properly used, the purchase record helps to control higher than necessary food and beverage costs.

Computerised purchasing systems

Some computer-generated purchase orders are produced by an integrated software package composed of numerous modules, one of which is the purchasing module. To generate accurate purchase orders, the purchasing module accesses data from other modules that maintain ingredient files, recipe files, menu item files, and inventory files.

Purchase orders can also be generated by a purchasing module that accesses and analyses unit sales forecast data. This method assumes a zerobased inventory system for developing purchasing orders. Rather than referencing existing inventory levels, the purchasing module forecasts anticipated unit sales, projects needed inventory items, and automatically generates the necessary purchase orders.

Regardless of the method used to produce purchase orders, purchasing modules typically provide override options that enable management to alter items and quantities prior to the final preparation and distribution of purchase orders. Properties dealing with more than one supplier may receive competitive bids and store them in a bid specification file that typically contains the specific characteristics of purchased items.

Suppliers are asked to quote prices for products that meet or exceed stated specifications. Normally, a bid specification form can be printed at any time upon demand. Once bids are obtained, they can be entered into the computer system, and the purchasing module can sort items to be purchased by supplier and lowest bid.

Telephone communication links between food service operations and suppliers are on the increase and have a significant impact on the ordering process. A growing trend among computer system vendors and food service suppliers is to install order entry telephone lines for telecommunicating purchase orders directly from customer properties. The property must first develop its own purchase order file and then use communications software to send purchase orders to the supplier's computer system. Purchase order filing is usually sorted by vendor and maintained by purchase order number and date.

Some suppliers allow clients to use auto dial modems. An autodial modem functions without user intervention, enabling late-night transmission of purchase orders for next -day processing. Some sophisticated purchase order telecommunication links provide for two-way communication (duplex) between the supplier and the property. This linkage allows the food and beverage purchaser to make online inquiries about current prices and/ or stock availability. It also permits the supplier to send information about featured items, price specials, and close-out sales to the purchaser. Today, some large food and beverage operations are developing computerised Just-In-Time (JIT) purchasing systems.

Managers at such operations realise that excess inventory ties up cash and valuable storage space, so they work with prime suppliers to develop JIT systems. Prime suppliers are suppliers who receive all-or a significant amount-of an operation's purchase orders for selected products during a specified time period. Prime suppliers are selected by comparing price quotations for the volume of estimated product quantities for specific time periods that are submitted by eligible suppliers.

By using one JIT plan, individual outlets within a property can calculate ingredients needed for daily production and electronically transmit those needs to the purchasing office, where totals of all ingredients required for the following day's preparation needs are assessed. These totals are then transmitted to the prime supplier, who delivers the needed products in time for preparation. Properties that use JIT systems require a relatively small amount of storage space for backup supplies because products are supplied according to need. As purchasing processes become increasingly computerised, implementation of JIT systems becomes more practical all the time.

Security Concerns in Purchasing

In small food and beverage operations, where owners/ managers may purchase and receive the products themselves, control procedures are less concerned with theft than with obtaining the best value. In larger operations, where other personnel take on purchasing tasks, security becomes an increasingly important concern. The control process must guard against several types of theft that are possible during the purchasing process.

— *Kickbacks.* In several common types of kickbacks, the buyer works in collusion with someone from the supplier's company. The kickback can be money or gifts. Either way, the owner of the operation is the loser. In one kickback scheme, products are purchased at prices higher than necessary. The two thieves then split the difference between the real and inflated prices. To best control this type of theft, the owner/ manager can routinely review invoices and ask such questions as, "Why are so many products purchased from the same supplier?"

The manager can also periodically review the selection of suppliers and solicit price quotations randomly to ensure that prices paid are the best-or, at least, competitive-for the requited product quantity. In another kickback procedure, the delivery invoice is padded by adding items that were not received, or it is increased by adding unreasonable charges for handling or some other service. This scheme works well when the same employee receives as well as purchases. Therefore, designing a system that separates the purchasing and receiving tasks can help prevent this type of kickback.

You have learned that, in large hotels, purchasing may be the responsibility of a staff purchasing department. Receiving and storing activities may be performed by the accounting department. Under this system, products do not come under the control of production staff until they are issued. This system helps reduce the possibility that one person, working alone, can implement a kickback scheme.

— *Fictitious Companies*. Purchasing personnel can steal by setting up a nonexistent company that then submits invoices for products never received. Managers can periodically review the selection of suppliers by examining the names of payees on company checks. Unless the manager is familiar with the supplier, checks should never be sent to companies with only post office box addresses.

— *Reprocessing*. Suppliers may try to send an invoice to the food and beverage operation for processing a second time. To avoid this type of theft, operations need an internal system to verify which invoices have not been paid and to cancel invoices when they are paid.

— *Delivery Invoice Errors*. Intentional arithmetic errors, short weight or counts, wrong quality, and similar" mistakes" can cost the operation money. Management or secretarial personnel must check all arithmetic on invoices and statements-even when they are computer-generated-and follow proper receiving practices to catch these mistakes. Whether they are innocent mistakes or fraud, the bottom line is the same: the operation loses money.

— *Credit Memo Problems.* When products are not delivered or when deliveries are short of the quantities ordered, a requestfor-credit memo should be issued to reduce the original delivery invoice by the value of the items not delivered. The supplier should then issue a credit memo to adjust the account. Managers and receiving staff should never accept a "we'll deliver it later and not charge you" comment from the truck driver. A request-for-credit memo should be written and attached to the delivery invoice. The manager should also alert the property's accounting department to ensure that the supplier properly processes the credit to the buyer's account.

— *Quality Substitutions.* Quality substitutions occur when a price is quoted for the proper quality item but a lower quality item is delivered. Proper receiving practices can prevent paying more for a lower quality product. Brand or label substitutions are also possible if receiving personnel are not familiar with products ordered. If alert staff do recognise product problems, the supplier can" allege" a mistake and exchange the products for those of proper quality. This problem occurs more frequently than some purchasers may suspect and requires close attention to both purchasing and receiving duties.

— *Purchaser Theft.* Purchasers might practice a variety of other thefts: purchasing for their own use, reciprocal purchasing for their own benefit, purchasing products wholesale with the intention of reselling them to selected employees or to others. Using an effectively designed purchasing system can help reduce these types of potential problems.

There is a gray area of purchasing ethics in which purchasing personnel may be offered gifts or free meals, invitations to parties, or other inducements designed to increase the supplier's business. Buyers must put the property first and make decisions based on what is best for the property rather than for themselves.

Reducing the Cost of the Purchasing Function

Professional food and beverage managers adopt a number of techniques to make certain that purchase dollars are spent wisely.

— *Negotiate Prices.* Some food and beverage managers mistakenly believe that an initial price quoted by the supplier is "fixed" and that purchasing involves simply soliciting price quotations and then accepting the lowest price quoted for the specified quality. In fact, discussions with sales managers (not the distributor sales representative who calls on the buyer) may yield lower prices.

— *Review Quality Standards.* Be sure that the proper quality of products is being purchased. If, for example, products of higher than necessary quality are being used, purchase prices can be reduced by purchasing items of the correct quality.

Evaluate the Need to Purchase Convenience Products

Sometimes, employees can prepare products of acceptable quality at a lower cost than that required for purchasing the products in a convenience form.

Discontinue Unnecessary Supplier Services. Costs incurred by suppliers for such services as storage, handling, delivery, and" grace" periods for the payment of bills may all be included in the product purchase cost. Purchasing staff should carefully consider exactly what services are desired and assess whether purchase prices can be reduced if other undesired services are discontinued.

Combine Orders. Sometimes purchase costs can be reduced if a larger order is placed with a supplier. The concept of "onestop" shopping, which involves buying a wide range of products from one supplier, recognises this principle.

Purchase in Larger Quantities. If practical, a larger number of units of required products can be purchased. It is necessary, of course, to weigh potential savings from volume purchases against costs incurred in tying up money and inventory space. With large volume purchases, there is also an increased possibility of theft and a potential increase in spoilage and other quality problems.

Pay Cash. Some suppliers will quote a lower price if products are paid for at the time of delivery.

Change Purchase Unit Size. For example, if flour is purchased in a 50-pound bag rather than a la-pound bag, the cost per pound is likely to be less.

Consider Cooperative Purchasing. Consider the use of cooperative (pool) purchasing, in which several properties combine orders to increase the volume of items ordered.

Consider Promotional Discounts. "Opportunity buys" (for example, items that a supplier plans to discontinue or has overstocked) sometimes arise,' and, if the products can be used by the operation, these can represent significant savings over regular prices.

Receiving Controls

The planning and control that goes into the purchasing process is wasted if no one ensures that products delivered meet the operation's standard purchase specifications. In too many operations, whoever happens to be "close to the back door" when a delivery is made signs the invoice. Great care must be taken to ensure an effective receiving process. Receiving is an important part of the product cost control system.

Receiving Personnel

Effective receiving requires knowledgeable receiving personnel. Staff must be trained to receive properly. They must know product quality standards and be able to recognise them when products are delivered. They must also understand all receiving procedures and know how to complete internal receiving records. The number of persons who receive products varies among food service operations. In a relatively small operation, the manager or the assistant manager may be in charge of receiving. In a larger operation, full-time or part-time staff typically handle the receiving function, and the person in charge of receiving may be called a receiving or storeroom clerk, or steward.

This individual usually reports to either the food controller, the assistant manager, or the food and beverage manager. Regardless of how many individuals are assigned to the receiving function, the general requirements are the same. Naturally, good health and personal cleanliness are essential for the receiver, as well as for all other personnel in the food service business. To protect the health of guests and employees alike, strict sanitation standards should be part of every aspect of food handling.

Receiving personnel should be able to use all required equipment, facilities, and forms. Because of the volume of written information to be processed, receiving staff must be able to read and write. Among other things, they must be able to check the actual products delivered against the written purchase specifications, written purchase orders, and the invoice itself.

Receiving personnel must be committed to protecting the interests of the operation. While food production experience is invaluable, this does not imply that any kitchen worker in the operation is qualified to perform the receiving function. Only selected and trained employees should be permitted to receive food and beverage products.

Properly trained receivers know what to do when there is a problem with product deliveries. In this respect, the receiving function is just as important as the purchasing function; as soon as the receiver signs the invoice, the merchandise legally becomes the property of the food and beverage operation and is no longer the responsibility of the supplier. Finally, receiving personnel need cooperation from other departments in the food service property or hotel. They must coordinate purchase requisitions from the departments with the delivery schedules of suppliers.

Ideally, receiving should take place during slow periods in the operation's daily business cycle. By scheduling deliveries at these times, the receiver's undivided attention can be given to the receiving duties. The property's delivery hours should be posted on the back door, and the receiver should always be available when deliveries are expected. A supplier's ability to accommodate an operation's delivery hours should be a major consideration in the supplier selection process.

The receiving area should be near the delivery door. Delivery personnel should be allowed only in restricted back-of-the house areas and should not be permitted in food production areas, access corridors, or other off-limits areas. Since proper receiving requires that most items be weighed or counted, accurate, conveniently located scales are necessary along with other equipment such as calculators, marking pens, rulers, files, thermometers, and transportation equipment.

Receiving Procedures

Control procedures adopted by food and beverage operations include the following:

Check Incoming Products against Purchase Orders or Purchase Records

Obviously, the property does not want to accept items it did not order, receive partial or no deliveries of required products, receive items of unacceptable quality, or pay a price higher than that agreed upon. These problems can be prevented by comparing incoming products against an inhouse record of the purchase agreement.

Check Incoming Products against Standard Purchase

This requires knowledgeable and skilled receiving personnel. They should not allow themselves to be rushed by delivery persons. Sometimes the suppliers will agree to deliver products at their risk, allowing the buyer to sign and send invoices after inspecting deliveries. Cooperation in receiving is an important item to consider when selecting suppliers. Whether receiving 96-count (to the case) lemons, chilled poultry, or fresh seafood, receiving staff must know how to confirm that the correct product is, in fact, being delivered and that the food and beverage operation is getting what it pays for.

Check Incoming Products against Delivery Invoices

The supplier provides the delivery invoice, which becomes the basis for subsequent payment claims. A definite policy must be developed, implemented, and enforced for the measuring, weighing, or counting of incoming products to ensure that the proper quantity of product is delivered and billed. Typically, it is not practical to weigh or count every case of product being delivered. It is helpful, however, to routinely weigh/ count selected cases on a random basis.

Suppliers or delivery persons are less likely to short-weigh a count if they expect random inspections. Likewise, price information on the invoice should be verified by reviewing the purchase order or purchase record. Any discrepancies should be handled by a request-for-credit memo.

— *Accept Incoming Products.* This is normally done by signing the delivery invoice. At this point, ownership of the products is transferred to the property, and the products become the responsibility of the food and beverage operation.

— *Move Accepted Products to Storage Immediately.* Security to minimise employee theft is a concern here. Likewise, the quality of products needing low-temperature storage will deteriorate if they are left at room temperatures, which are frequently very warm in back-of-the-house production areas. Use a stock rotation process; incoming items should be placed behind and/ or under items already in inventory.

— *Complete Necessary Receiving Documents.* The daily receiving report is used for several purposes:

  — To separate beverage costs-liquor, beer, wine, soda-from food costs. This information is needed for income statements that isolate revenue and" costs of goods sold" categories for these items.

  — To add up the value of "directs" in a daily food cost assessment system.

  — To transfer responsibility for product control from receiving to storeroom personnel (in large operations with different receiving and storeroom personnel).

Request-for-Credit Memos

Every time a delivery invoice is modified at the time of receiving, a request for credit memo becomes necessary. For example, if deliveries do not include the full quantity specified on the delivery invoice, are refused because of quality problems, or are rejected for any other reason, this is noted on the request for-credit memo. Never permit the delivery person to leave off items on the invoice and deliver them" free" next time. The following procedures should be used to process a request-for-credit memo.

— Note problems with items on the invoice.

— Complete the request-for-credit memo, have the delivery person sign it, and return a copy to the supplier along with the delivery invoice.

— Attach the property's copy of the memo to its copy of the delivery invoice. Note the correct amount of the invoice on the face of the invoice.

— Call the supplier to advise that the original invoice has been amended by a request-for-credit memo.

— If short or refused products are subsequently delivered, a separate invoice can accompany the items. The new invoice is processed in the usual manner.

— Do not file any problem invoices. Hold them in a separate file until all problems, such as a supplier's confirmation of a credit, are resolved.

Marking Procedures

Marking and tagging puts invoice information directly on items. For example, marking case goods or bottles of liquor with the delivery date and price makes it easier to judge whether stock rotation plans are effective. Also, when valuing inventory, cost data can be taken directly from the cases or bottles; this saves the time needed to look up the information on the daily receiving report, delivery invoice, or in the computerised database. Recording the unit price on products makes it more likely that the operation's staff members will think about them as alternative forms of cash. Therefore, they may be more careful in handling, portioning, and controlling waste.

Security Concerns in Receiving

Example for supplier theft possibilities when products are received include the following.

— The supplier may deliver lesser quality items, such as inexpensive domestic wines instead of higher quality wines, or 30 percent fat content ground beef instead of 20 per cent, and the operation pays the price for the higher quality.

— Short-weight or short-count products may be delivered so the food service operation pays for more products than it receives.

— Thawed products may be represented as fresh, while the operation pays the higher price for fresh.

— Ice may be ground into ground meat products, fillers such as soy products or non-fat dry milk extenders may be added, and meat may be sold with excess fat trim.

— Weight of ice and/or packaging may be included in the product weight on which price is based.

— "Slacked out" seafood-frozen fish, thawed and packed in icemay be sold as fresh.

— Expensive steaks and inexpensive meat may be combined in one container, and when the entire container is weighed, the operation may be billed for more expensive steaks than are actually in the container.

— One empty liquor bottle may be included in a case of 12 bottles.

These are just a few of the many ways that suppliers can steal from the property by overcharging for amount and/ or quality. To help guard against theft at receiving, some basic principles should be followed:

— Have different people receive and purchase, unless the owner/manager performs both duties.

— Train employees to receive properly. Receiving is too important to leave to whomever happens to be handy.

— To the maximum extent possible, schedule product deliveries at slow times so that receiving personnel, who may have other duties, have time to receive correctly.

— Have deliveries made to a specified area of the facility, and be sure receiving scales and other equipment are available and are used.

— After receipt, immediately move products to storage.

Chances for employee theft increase the longer products remain unattended.

— Do not permit salespersons or delivery / route persons access to back-of-the house production or storage areas. To the maximum extent possible, the receiving area should be close to an outside exit and visible to management personnel.

— Lock the outside door. Install an audio signal so delivery persons can ring when they arrive. With this plan, receiving personnel have delivery persons in sight during their entire visit.

Computerised Receiving Systems

Computer technology is now helping some food and beverage operations with the receiving task. Over time, many additional properties will take advantage of technology as products are received. Packing cases containing food and beverage products often have universal product codes/bar code information attached. Data indicates product code (name), purchase/ delivery date, product price and, perhaps, other information. An optical scanner is used to "read" this information and, at the same time, update perpetual inventory levels and develop daily receiving and other reports desired by the operation. This process allows for rapid generation of important control information with minimal chances of error.

10

Inventory Controls

Food and beverage managers must recognise that product costs and quality are affected by storing and issuing systems. Unfortunately, many food and beverage operations lack adequate control procedures for these functions. Products are simply put in the storeroom when received and taken out when needed. Actually, food and beverage managers would do well to think of the storeroom as a bank vault. Products in storage represent money. If the storeroom contains, for example, $5,000 worth of food and beverage products, think of it as having 5,000 onedollar bills in storage. Stored products represent money in terms of both their initial cost as well as the cost to replace them if they are stolen, spoiled, or damaged because of improper storage practices. The same care and concern that go into procedures for controlling stored cash should also go into the procedures for controlling stored foods and beverages.

There are many reasons why strict storage and issuing controls are needed in food and beverage operations. Products can be stolen when issued from storage to production areas. Also, mistakes in issuing can result in more products being used in production than are necessary. This, in turn, can result in waste and unnecessarily high food or beverage costs. Moreover, since systems of assessing daily food and beverage costs are based, in part, on the value of daily issues, it is essential to know exactly how much of each product leaves storage areas.

Procedures of Storing Control

It is important to move food and beverage products into storage areas as soon as they are received. In addition, delivery personnel should have only limited access to back-of-the-house areas. This means that staff from the property-not the delivery persons-should be responsible for this transfer to storage. If deliveries are left unattended in receiving areas, refrigerated and frozen products can easily deteriorate in quality, and dishonest employees may have opportunities to steal. As soon as received products are moved to and placed in storage areas, their quality and security can be better ensured by the control procedures built into the property's storage system. The principles of effective storage systems for both food and beverage products focus on three primary concerns:

— Keeping products secure from theft

— Retaining product quality

— Providing information necessary for the financial accounting system Inventory Control Policy

When designing storage systems, every control procedure must be cost-effective. It is generally not practical for managers to attempt to regulate all food and beverage products under a strict system of tight controls. Some properties, for example, may not be able to justify a perpetual inventory system for any but the most expensive items. As a result, many food and beverage operations, especially smaller ones, maintain tight control over meats, seafood, liquor, and wine, but not as much control over less expensive and less theft-prone products.

Limited Access

Only authorised staff members should be permitted in storerooms. In addition to management, authorised staff in larger properties may include receiving and or storage personnel. Smaller operations can keep storage areas locked and involve management directly in receiving and issuing activities. When a manager is present to unlock the storeroom door, employee theft is less likely. This procedure is more easily implemented if issuing is done only at specified times.

Lockable Storage Areas

The storeroom, freezer, and beverage storage areas should be completely lockable. Depending upon available equipment, one section of a walk-in or reach-in refrigerator might be used to secure expensive refrigerated items. Or, a lockable shelving unit (or cage) can be kept in the walk-in refrigerator. In this way, expensive refrigerated products, such as fresh meats and seafood, or wines being chilled for service, can be kept secure from theft. At the same time, personnel can still have access to produce, dairy, and similar products that are less likely to be stolen.

Refrigerator freezer units should be lockable with reasonably strong lock clasps and door hinges. Storeroom walls should extend to the ceiling, and there should be no way to enter through the ceiling from another room. If there are windows, they should at least be made secure and unopenable. The point is to design, within practical limits, storage areas that are difficult for unauthorised employees to enter without being detected. Some properties maintain a "precious room." A precious room is a locked storage area within a locked storage area. For example, liquor and expensive buffet chafing dishes might be kept locked in a closet inside a locked storeroom. The goal of all of these procedures is to reduce opportunities for employee pilferage.

Behind-the-Bar Storage

The quantity of beverage products kept behind the bar should be minimal since storage space is limited and this area is less secure than the central storage area. Liquor should be locked behind the bar when the bar is closed. Lockable cabinets, rolldown screens, or similar devices can keep beverages out of the reach of cleaning staff and other employees when the bar is closed.

Storeroom Key Control

Only staff members who need keys should have them. Manual locks or combinations should be change routinely and each time an employee with access to keys leaves the property's employment. An excellent policy is that all keys remain at the property at all times, securely locked in the manager's office when not in use. Some food and beverage managers may feel key control procedures are unnecessary.

However, a significant number of dollars can be lost because of inadequate key control. This fact should convince managers to emphasize this aspect of the operation's control system. Newer locking systems eliminate the need for traditional keys. For example, pins correlating with a "combination code" can be depressed by authorised personnel who have memorised the code.

When these individuals no longer need access to lockable areas, combinations can be quickly (and inexpensively) changed. Other systems may use plastic cards, similar to credit cards, with coded information designed to operate locks. These systems are in common use for hotel guest rooms and are increasingly being used in back-of-house areas as well. Either of these or related systems may yield information about the identity of persons entering lockable areas, time of entry, and length of time that the individual was in the area. Increasingly, these and related systems provide more specific control information to help ensure that only persons authorised to enter storage areas do, in fact, gain access to these locations.

Quality during Storage

Improper storage practices can reduce the quality of products in storage. In fact, most food products including frozen foods experience a loss in quality if stored too long. While this is especially true for foods, it also applies to some wines and most beers. It is important that control procedures designed to minimise the loss of quality of products in storage be strictly followed. Food costs increase as items judged unfit for use are discarded and replaced. If, because of pressure to keep food costs down, lower quality products are served to guests, there may be serious marketing implications. The following are the present several procedures for maintaining quality during storage.

Product Rotation

The first-in, first-out (FIFO) inventory rotation method is a good rule. The products held in inventory the longest should be the first to be issued to production areas. To facilitate this, when newly received products enter storage areas they should be placed under or behind products already in storage. Marking the date of receipt on every item makes it possible to compare dates of products used in production with those of items in storage areas. Those items in production should have been received earlier than those remaining in storage.

This method will help management ensure that stock rotation practices are followed.

Properly Controlled Environment

Maintain proper temperature, humidity, and ventilation. Use accurate thermometers and check them routinely. Proper temperatures are (unless otherwise regulated by government sources):

— Dry storage temperature-SO ° to 70°F (10° to 21°C)

— Refrigerated storage temperature-40°F (4°C) or lower

— Freezer storage temperature-O°F (-18°C) or lower

Require management's permission to discard spoiled items. This way, managers can judge the effectiveness of its quality control methods and also assess the costs of failing to comply with proper storage procedures.

Sanitation Practices

Establish and follow regular cleaning times for all storage facilities, in contrast with cleaning them only when extra time becomes available. This applies not only to storerooms and storage spaces, but also to walk-in and reach-in refrigerators and storage equipment. Facilities and equipment should be made of nonporous, easily cleaned materials. Shelving units should be louvered or slotted to permit air circulation. They should not be covered with aluminium foil or any other material that impedes airflow. Lower shelves, drainage racks, and similar storage equipment should be at least two inches from walls and at least six inches off the floor to permit mop and broom cleaning and to discourage rodent and insect nesting.

In following proper sanitation practices, it is important to use professional pest control services. Faced with the many exotic chemicals and poisons on the market, probably very few food and beverage managers are qualified to plan and manage rodent and insect control programmes. It is too dangerous for a well-intentioned but untrained person to spray and spread chemicals in food production and service areas.

Proper Storage

Store products properly. For example, store products in their original packaging, away from the wall, to allow air circulation. Store items that absorb odors, such as flour, away from products that give off odors, such as onions. Store opened products in clean, labeled, covered containers designed for food storage, rather than using empty glass jars (which can break) or empty number-10 cans (which cannot be properly cleaned).

Generally, products should be stored in quantities that can be used within a reasonable time period. There are exceptions to this rule, such as investments in wines and volume purchases made as hedges against price increases, but these decisions should be made by top management, not by purchasing staff. Beverage products are generally stored for less than one month. Food items classified as stores are usually used within an even shorter time period. Perishable products are purchased two or more times weekly.

Inventory Control Procedures

The third major concern in storage, after security and minimising quality losses, is record keeping. We have already mentioned that inventory procedures play an important role in the security concerns of the control system. There are several other reasons for designing and implementing effective inventory record keeping systems:

— Financial accounting systems need inventory values to generate monthly statements. The value of products in inventory is considered part of the property's current assets (for the balance sheet) and is also used to assess costs (for the income statement).

— Daily control procedures may require knowing the quantity of products currently available. For example, a food and beverage manager may wish to keep a perpetual inventory record of selected expensive items to allow frequent and quick assessment of any differences between the quantities that should be in storage and how much is actually there.

— Inventory records help managers determine not only when to order new products, but also how much of each product to order.

Inventory Turnover

One important function of keeping accurate inventory records is to allow managers to assess how much money is being invested in nonproductive inventory. The value of goods in inventory is typically calculated on a monthly basis to provide information for financial accounting systems. Nonproductive inventory refers to products in storage that are not issued to production areas during the time period (usually monthly) covered by financial records. In order to determine how much money is tied up in nonproductive inventory, managers measure the inventory turnover rate. The inventory turnover rate shows the number of times in a given period that inventory is converted or turned into revenue. In financial terms, it measures the rate at which inventory is turned into food or-beverage costs required to generate food or beverage revenue.

Inventory turnover rates can be determined for food or beverage products in storage. The inventory turnover is calculated by dividing the cost of food (or beverages) used by the average food (or beverage) inventory (in dollars). The average inventory value is determined by adding the value of inventory at the beginning of the time period in question (usually a month) to the value of inventory at the end of that period and then dividing the sum by two.

For example, to calculate the inventory turnover rate for food products for a month, assume the following data:

— Food Inventory Value at Beginning of Month = $18,500

— Food Inventory Value at End of Month = $19,500

— Cost of Food Used = $122,750

The inventory turnover rate is an important tool to use in managing inventory levels. As this rate decreases, more money is being invested in inventory. If too much of the property's funds are being used to purchase excess products for inventory, cash flow problems may result and create other difficulties for the operation. Also, products may spoil or otherwise deteriorate in quality because of excessive inventory levels. On the other hand, as the turnover rate increases, less money is being invested in inventory. As average inventory levels are reduced, however, a point will be reached at which stockouts begin to occur and guest dissatisfaction and operating problems can result.

Therefore, to properly control the property's investment in inventory, food and beverage managers must determine the best turnover rate for their particular operations. This process requires monitoring. If the turnover rate is calculated monthly, the food and beverage manager can learn of any increases or decreases in inventory turnover and respond accordingly. It may also be a good idea to calculate turnover rates for specific product categories. One would normally expect highly perishable items (such as fresh meats and seafood, fruits, and vegetables) to turn over more rapidly than less perishable items (such as spices, staples, and frozen or canned products).

Inventory Recordkeeping Systems

There are two basic kinds of recordkeeping systems for products in storage: physical inventory and perpetual inventory. A physical inventory system involves actual observation and counting of stored products on a periodic basis. A perpetual inventory system involves keeping a running balance of the quantity of stored products by recording all newly purchased items as they enter storage areas and all quantities issued from storage to production areas.

Physical Inventory System

A physical inventory system is used to periodically assess the value of food and beverage products in inventory. This is done at least monthly to develop information needed for the balance sheet and income statement. Inventory value is counted as a current asset, and inventory values, both at the beginning and end of the financial period, are a factor in assessing food and beverage costs. Before a physical inventory of stored products can be taken, the food and beverage manager must make several decisions about the design of the physical inventory system.

— What products should be considered in making an inventory count. This decision is partially related to the question of which areas are to be considered storage areas under the control of the inventory system. For example, does inventory include products in broken-case and workstation storage areas? What about products in process, such as frozen poultry thawing in the refrigerator? What items are" stores" and included in inventory, and what items are" directs" and excluded from inventory?

— How should monetary value be assigned to products in inventory. One method is to calculate the actual cost of stored products at the time the physical inventory is made. Another method is to use the average costs of stored products over several inventory counts. Others include the last-in, first-out (LIFO) inventory valuation system and the first-in, first-out (FIFO) inventory valuation system. Under the LIFO system, the costs of the products most recently added to inventory (last in) are the costs assigned when products are issued (first out). This leads to cost of sales figures that more accurately reflect current replacement costs. It also tends to create a smaller total inventory value. That is, since the most recent (and usually most expensive) costs are the first to be "issued," the remaining inventory is made up of the earlier (and usually lower) costs. Conversely, under the FIFO system, the oldest (and usually lowest) costs are" issued" first, leaving the more recent (and usually higher) costs remaining in inventory. This creates a higher total inventory value and a lower cost of sales. Typically, an accountant helps determine the best inventory valuation system for the property. This is because inventory values affect food costs, which impact profitability and, therefore, taxes.

— How should costs of such items as opened containers of spices in production areas and opened bottles of liquor at the bar be handled. Often, the cost of such opened, unused items is assumed to average out. In other words, their value is thought to remain approximately the same from month to month. So, once an estimated cost is established, it can be used monthly.

— What procedures should be used in counting the products in inventory? Persons involved in managing storage areas should not take inventory counts alone. Perhaps the food inventory can be taken by the food manager, while the beverage manager takes the beverage inventory. In both situations, a representative from the accounting office can assist in conducting the physical inventory.

A physical inventory indicates only how much of each product is in inventory and the actual value of all stored products. Two limitations of a physical inventory system are that it does not indicate how much of each product should be available and what the value of products in inventory should be. A perpetual inventory system compensates for these problems.

Perpetual Inventory System

A perpetual inventory system keeps a running balance of the quantity of food and beverage products in inventory. It operates like a bank checking account. When more food or beverages are put in the bank (the storage area), the balance is increased. As products are removed (issued), the balance decreases. At any time, then, the amount of products that should be currently available is known.

Large properties with specialised storage and accounting personnel may use a perpetual inventory system for all, or almost all, products in storage. Small food and beverage operations may find it more practical to use perpetual inventory control only for expensive items and those purchased in large quantities.

A physical count is still necessary with a perpetual inventory system to verify the accuracy of the inventory balances. When using a perpetual inventory system, staff members who maintain the perpetual inventory records should not perform the physical inventory used for verification.

When the physical count of a product differs from the quantity indicated on the perpetual record, a control problem may exist, and management must determine the reason for the variance. Perhaps products are not being recorded at the time of receipt or issue, or perhaps theft is occurring. The purpose of control procedures is to indicate when such problems exist. Management' s task is to discover why a problem exists and, of course, to correct it.

Computerised Inventory Management

Despite its obvious importance, inventory control is one of the least uniform software applications. Systems differ in file capacity and report capability. Moreover, the food and beverage business, with its unique inventory characteristics, usually does not lend itself to using software developed for another industry. In other words, if an automobile manufacturer, a bicycle repair shop, and a retail clothing chain can successfully use the same inventory control package, this does not mean that the software can be used successfully in a food and beverage operation.

Ideally, the software will feature an integrated package containing an ingredient file (for food and non-food items) and an inventory file. The ingredient file contains all necessary information to define the ingredients. The inventory file deals with inventory stock levels and reorder points and is used for computing usage, variances, and product valuations. The initial creation of a food and beverage ingredient file and subsequent file updates (daily, weekly, monthly, etc.) can be an overwhelming task for some food service operations. For example, a restaurant may offer 30 (or more) food items and 50 (or more) beverage products. An inventory of 1,500 ingredients may need to be purchased. If errors are made when data is initially entered, all subsequent processing will be unreliable and system reports will be relatively worthless. In addition, computer applications that do not support integrated files can be extremely cumbersome because users must re-input data from several files to run a particular programme.

Some inventory applications provide file space for more than one ingredient designation, such as item file code number, inventory sequence number, internal customer code, and so on. The ability to work with additional designations can increase the efficiency of the inventory control system. For example, a user may be able to print ingredients on a physical inventory worksheet according to the order in which they are shelved.

Another concern is how usage is charted by the inventory application-by unit, by cost, or by both unit and cost. A system that charts items by unit may be able to report changes in stock levels, but may not be able to provide financial data necessary for food costing. The most effective inventory applications are those that track items in terms of both unit and cost.

Conversion tables can be maintained by which to track ingredients (by unit and by cost) as they pass through purchasing/ receiving, storing/issuing, and production/ service control points. To efficiently maintain a perpetual inventory record, a computerised inventory management system must be able to automatically convert purchase units into issue units and recipe units (also referred to as usable units). Inventory data must be specific to each of these control points because purchase units (i.e., case, drum, etc.) may differ from storeroom inventory units. Storeroom inventory units, in turn, differ from standard recipe units (i.e., ounce, cup, etc.).

Some systems are not able to support the number of conversion tables necessary to track menu items through ingredient purchase, storage, and use (standard recipe). For example, assume that an ingredient is purchased, issued, and used in different units. When a shipment of the ingredient arrives, it should be easy to update the inventory record by simply entering the purchase unit received. The computer should then automatically convert this entry into issue units.

Without this conversion capability, it would be necessary to manually calculate the number of units that will be stored and increase the inventory record accordingly. Similarly, at the end of a meal period, the computer system should be capable of updating the inventory record by entering the standard recipe units that should have been used to prepare menu items.

If the restaurant management system cannot convert issue units into recipe units, these calculations may also have to be performed manually and the inventory record decreased accordingly. Similarly, the computer-based system should also be able to track the costs associated with these various ingredient units. For example, assume that ketchup is purchased by the case (six number-l0 cans), issued from the storeroom to the kitchen by the can, and used in recipes by the ounce. Given the information about the purchase unit's net weight and cost, the computer should be able to automatically extend costs for issue and recipe unit(s).

To arrive at these costs through manual calculations, an employee must compute the price per ounce of the purchase unit. Performing these calculations manually for every ingredient purchased can be a tedious, error-prone, timeconsuming process. A food service management applications package can perform these calculations in fractions of a second. Care must be taken to ensure that the ingredient file contains the necessary data and conversion definitions.

Management should clarify how basic food service concepts are defined within the inventory application design. While the terms "inventory usage," "inventory variance," and" inventory valuation" are common, they do not have the same meaning in all computer systems. For example, inventory usage attempts to identify changes in inventory level (depletion of stock on hand) from one point in time to another.

However, is an inventory item considered "used" (for costing purposes) at the time it is received, or when it is issued to the kitchen, or at the time of service? Each of these time frames presents a different usage result and subsequent cost computation. The point in time that is most desirable for a particular restaurant operation may not be the time frame that is built into the application's design. Also, since methods of inventory valuation vary, management must be careful to clarify which methods a particular food service inventory package should support.

Technology can also assist in the inventory valuation process through optical scanning. Universal product code (UPC) information on product packages can be scanned to quickly and accurately assess the quantity of unopened product packages in inventory. Scanning results can provide helpful information for verifying perpetual inventories and for calculating cost-ofgoods-sold data when actual food and beverage costs are calculated.

Beverage Inventory

The basic control procedures already noted apply to both food and beverage products. However, since beverages, especially liquor and wine, are expensive and popular targets of theft, they require some special control precautions. Even small food and beverage operations normally use a perpetual inventory system for alcoholic beverages. While important for many stored food products, control procedures such as locked storage areas, controlled access, and management of storeroom access are especially critical to the control of alcoholic beverages. The inventory task is easier if prices are marked on the bottles or cases when they are originally placed in storage.

An important consideration in designing inventory control procedures for beverages is whether beverage inventory values will include items currently behind the bar as well as beverage items in the central storeroom. Consistency is the key here. Items behind the bar should either always be included or never be included in inventory recordkeeping procedures.

Some beverage managers believe it is unnecessary to include items behind the bar in inventories because the bar quantities will average out. Others believe that the increased accuracy gained from including behind-the-bar items in inventory records, and the tighter control this provides, is worthwhile. If only central storeroom beverage products are to be counted, the physical inventory form is sufficient for recording information about quantities and costs. This inventory form can, then, be used for both food and beverage items. However, when both central storeroom and behind-the-bar inventory costs are assessed, a beverage inventory cost card can be used.

Behind-the-bar inventory costs

When beverage items behind the bar are valued for inventory purposes, the following procedures can be used to manually assess costs:

— Count the number of unopened bottles of each type of beverage product.

— Determine the quantity of beverage products in opened bottles. This can be done either by visually estimating (for example, to the nearest tenth of a bottle), by weighing, or by using dipsticks.

— Add the number of unopened bottles of each type of beverage to the amount remaining in opened bottles to assess the total volume of product available behind the bar.

— Add the amount in the central storeroom to the behind-the bar amount to determine the total beverage inventory.

— Calculate the total cost .of beverage items in inventory.

Computerised scales

Computerised scales are now available to accurately weigh open bottles of alcoholic beverages behind the bar when taking beverage inventories. The process is simple: each type of liquor (for example, a 750 ml bottle of house Scotch or a specific size bottle of a call brand) is given a code. This code indicates the empty bottle weight. The person taking inventory places an opened bottle on the scale and enters the code into the computer. The computer then (a) deducts the empty bottle weight from the total open bottle weight, (b) determines the quantity of liquor available in the bottle, and (c) calculates the cost of liquor and sales value of each type of liquor in behind-the-bar storage areas. Use of a computerised scale improves the speed and accuracy of taking inventory.

Issuing control

At some point, products are removed from storage and transferred to production areas-the kitchen and bar. Unfortunately, some properties have very informal, if any, issuing procedures and exert little control over this process. An open door policy may even be in effect:

whenever anyone needs something, they simply walk into the storage area and take it.

However, if a food and beverage operation does not limit access, to storage areas and keep records of items removed, it is not possible to compare the quantity of products removed from storage with the quantity of items produced or the levels of revenue generated. Limited access to storage areas and special procedures for issuing products from storage to production are essential for effective food and beverage controls. When designing basic control procedures for a food and beverage operation, it is important to consider this aspect of the management system.

The objectives of an effective issuing system can be met by using techniques available to food and beverage operations of all sizes. A well-designed issuing system has the following objectives:

- To limit access to storage areas to authorised staff members only.
- To match items removed from storage with actual production requirements.
- To assess quantities and costs of products removed from storage.

This record keeping becomes important when updating perpetual inventory records and assessing costs of issues to calculate daily food and beverage costs.

Issuing procedures

Any food and beverage operation, regardless of size, can make use of requisition forms. Large hotels and restaurants often have full-time storeroom staff who assemble products included on requisitions and sign them over to production unit employees. Smaller properties may assign issuing responsibilities to employees who work in storerooms at specified times only. All of these methods succeed in limiting access to storage areas and assigning responsibility for issuing to a specific person.

In addition, the requisition forms can be used to provide information for daily cost calculations or to update perpetual inventory records. Thus, there are reasonable procedures that any food and beverage operation can develop to properly control issuing procedures. By planning ahead, issuing can be limited to specified times. For example, products for making breakfast might be issued from 6:00 to 6:30 A.M. Items needed for lunch could be issued from 10:30 to 11:00 A.M., and similarly for dinner or late evening shifts. Normally, beverages to replenish bar inventories are issued either at the beginning or end of each bar shift.

Computer-generated issue quantities

Precost computer software enables management to apply a projected sales mix across a standard recipe file to produce a "prior to service" cost report. A byproduct of this costing scheme is a complete list of all ingredient quantities required to satisfy the demand for a planned menu. In other words, if four items on a given menu each require ketchup as a recipe ingredient, the quantity of ketchup to be issued would be the total amount for the entire meal period. Ingredient totals are typically contained in a breakout quantities report. The computer system lists all items (by issue unit) requiring requisition to produce a projected sales mix.

Requisition information is electronically transferred from user departments to the storage area(s). No "paperwork" is required. Some software packages go a step further and split breakout quantities by preparation area. In this case, ingredients are summed by preparation area only (found in each recipe record) and reported accordingly. Therefore, although the fryer, broiler, and pantry stations may all use the same ingredient, individual breakout lists will contain only the appropriate total for each workstation. This approach helps tighten inventory control and, over time, may provide a basis for a highly reliable forecasting system. Projected sales mixes, which! yield breakout quantities, are easily assessed based on whether sufficient quantities were issued.

— If secondary requisitioning is necessary, the forecasting formulas must be refined.

— The Beverage Requisition/Issue Process

— The basic procedures for issuing food also apply to beverages.

However, since beverages, by their nature, are very susceptible to employee theft, there are several additional concerns in transferring beverages from storage to production areas. Special procedures incorporated into beverage issuing can reduce the possibility or frequency of employee theft.

Establishing bar par inventory levels

Beverages should be issued only in quantities needed to reestablish bar par inventory levels. A bar par is an established number of bottles of each type of beverage that is always kept in behind-the-bar storage areas. A bar par is established for each type of liquor and wine kept behind the bar. Some food and beverage operations also set pars for bottled beer. Bar pars are established on the basis of the number of bottles of each beverage type used during a busy shift. For example, if an average busy shift uses four bottles of house brand Scotch, the beverage manager may be conservative and set the bar par at five bottles-four full bottles in behind-the-bar storage and one opened bottle in the speedrail or back-bar display area.

The number of empty bottles at the beginning or end of each shift-preferably the end-determines the number of full bottles needed to replenish the bar par. If, for example, the bar par is five bottles for house Scotch and two bottles are empty, then two bottles will be issued to maintain the bar par. An important rule is that empty bottles must be presented before full bottles are issued.

Beverage issuing steps

The beverage issuing process typically includes the following steps:

- At the end of each shift, the bartender places the bottles emptied during the shift on top of the bar.
- The bartender completes a beverage requisition form, recording the name of each type of liquor or wine emptied, the number of empty bottles, and the size of the bottle. Depending upon the specific property, the bartender may also record the unit cost. Information for this column comes from the invoice cost marked on the bottle at the time it was placed in storage.
- The beverage manager checks the number and type of empty bottles on the bar against the information on the beverage requisition form. If there are no problems, he or she signs or initials the" OK to Issue" section of the sheet.
- The bartender or manager takes the empty bottles and the beverage requisition to the beverage storage area. The person responsible for issuing: (a) compares empty bottles with the data on the issue requisition, (b) bottle for bottle, replaces empty bottles with full ones, and (c) signs or initials the "issued by" section of the sheet. At the same time, the bartender or manager, who returns full bottles to the bar, signs or initials the" received by" section.

— Empty bottles are broken or otherwise disposed of according to local or state laws, or as specified by the property's control requirements designed to prevent reuse.

— Total cost calculations and the beverage cost percent calculations at the bottom of the requisition form are normally completed by management or secretarial/ bookkeeping personnel, not the bartender or storeroom issuing staff. Except in large properties with storeroom personnel, management office staff should maintain perpetual inventory records for beverage products.

Bottle marking

Bottle marking identifies a bottle before it is issued. It may simply identify the bottle as house property, or it may also contain information about the bottle's cost and/ or date of issue. If, however, there is more than one bar in a property, bottles should additionally be marked with the site to which it is issued.

Frequently, the bottle mark is an adhesive-backed label or hard to-remove ink stamp, with a logo or symbol difficult to duplicate. Since the bottle mark identifies the bottle as house property, it helps supervisory staff ensure that all bottles behind the bar belong to the property. There is less likelihood that bartenders can bring in bottles and steal from the operation by selling their own liquor and keeping the revenue.

Bottle marking is important for two other reasons. First, if the cost, from the daily receiving report or delivery invoice, is recorded on the bottle, it is easier to complete the issue requisition form. Second, if the date of issue is recorded on the bottle, it is easier to keep track of the rotation of bottles behind the bar.

The bottle mark, or at least the cost and date of issue, should not be easy to notice. Sometimes special situations require making exceptions to bottle-marking practices. Bottles going to the table, such as liquor for flaming and wine, might be marked on the bottom.

Finally, several additional control concerns about issuing beverages should be noted. When beverages behind the bar frequently run out, bar par levels must be re-examined and increased. Guests do not want to wait while another bottle is brought from the storeroom. Similarly, there may not be time to complete a beverage issue requisition in the middle of a rush period, so information about beverage costs and reduced perpetual inventory balances is lost. To avoid these problems, managers should carefully assess the need for behind-the-bar inventories during the operation's busy periods, and issuing times and bar par quantities should be planned accordingly.

When the bar is not in operation, all bar par inventories should be locked to discourage employee theft. In addition, keys to beverage storeroom areas should not be left with bartenders. In small operations, the key can be sealed in an envelope placed behind the bar. If it must be used when a manager is not immediately available, it will be available. However, the opened envelope will show that the storeroom has been entered. An immediate comparison of perpetual inventory records with physical count may then be in order.

11

Managing Food Revenue and Expense

The goal of restaurant revenue management (RRM) is to maximise revenue per available seat hour (RevPASH) by manipulating price and meal duration. Restaurant revenue management can be defined as selling the right seat to the right customer at the right price and for the right duration. The determination of "right" entails achieving both the most revenue possible for the restaurant and also delivering the greatest value or utility to the customer.

Revenue management, or yield management, is commonly practiced in the airline industry and, to a somewhat lesser degree, the lodging industry. Companies implementing revenue management report increases in revenue of 2 to 5 percent over the results of prior procedures.

Restaurant operators can manipulate two main strategic levers to manage revenue: price and meal duration. Price is a fairly obvious target for manipulation, and many operators already offer price-related promotions to augment or shift peak-period demand (e.g., early bird specials, special menu promotions). More-sophisticated manipulations of price include day-part pricing, day-of-week pricing, and price premiums or discounts based on party or table size.

Managing meal duration (i.e., speeding table turns) is a bit more complicated, as we discuss in a moment. For example, meal duration depends in part on the efficiency of the restaurant's service cycle, as well as on the idiosyncrasies of customer-arrival patterns and diners' deciding to linger (or not) after the meal.

ROLE OF PROFESSIONAL FOODSERVICE MANAGER

There is no doubt that to be a successful foodservice manager you must be a talented individual. Consider, for a moment, your role in the operation of an ongoing profitable facility. As a foodservice manager, you are both a manufacturer and a retailer. A professional foodservice manager is unique because all of the functions of product sales, from item conceptualisation to product delivery, are in the hands of the same individual.

As a manager, you are in charge of securing raw materials producing a product, and selling it-all under the same roof. Few other managers are required to have the breadth of skills that effective foodservice operators must have. Because foodservice operators are in the service sector of business, many aspects of management are more difficult for them than for their manufacturing or retailing management counterparts.

A foodservice manager is one of the few types of managers who actually have contact with the ultimate customer. This is not true of the manager of a tire factory or automobile production line. These individuals produce a product, but they do not sell it to the person who will actually use their product. In a like manner, grocery store or computer store managers will sell their product lines, but they have had no role in actually producing their goods. The face-to-face guest contact in the hospitality industry requires that you assume the responsibility of standing behind your own work and that of your staff, in a one-on-one situation with the ultimate consumer, or end user of your products and services.

In addition to your role as a food factory supervisor, you must also serve as a cost control manager, because, without performing this vital role, your business might cease to exist. Foodservice management provides the opportunity for creativity in a variety of settings. The control of revenue and expense is just one more area in which the effective foodservice operator can excel. In most areas of foodservice, excellence in operation is measured in terms of producing and delivering quality products in a way that assures an appropriate operating profit for the owners of the business.

Profit

There is an inherent problem in the study of cost control or, more accurately, cost management. The simple fact is that management's primary responsibility is to deliver a quality product or service to the guest, at a price mutually agreeable to both parties. In addition, the quality must be such that the consumer, or end user of the product or service, feels that excellent value was received for the money spent on the transaction. When this level of service is achieved, the business will prosper. If management focuses on controlling costs more than servicing guests, problems will certainly surface.

It is important to remember that guests cause businesses to incur costs. You do not want to get yourself in the mind-set of reducing costs to the point where it is thought that "low" costs are good and "high" costs are bad. A restaurant with $5 million in revenue per year will undoubtedly have higher costs than the same size restaurant with $200,000 in revenue per year. The reason is quite clear. The food products, labour, and equipment needed to sell $5 million worth of food is likely to be greater than that required to produce a smaller amount of revenue.

Remember, if there are fewer guests, there are likely to be fewer costs, but fewer profits as well! Because that is true, when management attempts to reduce costs, with no regard for the impact on the balance between managing costs and guest satisfaction, the business will surely suffer. In addition, efforts to reduce costs that result in unsafe conditions for guests or employees are never wise.

While some shortterm savings may result, the expense of a lawsuit resulting from a guest or employee injury can be very high. Managers who, for example, neglect to spend the money to salt and shovel a snowy restaurant entrance area may find that they spend thousands more dollars defending themselves in a lawsuit brought by an individual who slipped and fell on the ice.

As an effective manager, the question to be considered is not whether costs are high or low. The question is whether costs are too high or too low, given management's view of the value it hopes to deliver to the guest and the goals of the foodservice operation's owners. Managers can eliminate nearly all costs by closing the operation's doors. Obviously, however, when you close the doors to expense, you close the doors to profits. Expenses, then, must be incurred, and they must be managed in a way that allows the operation to achieve its desired profit levels.

Some people assume that if a business purchases a product for $1.00 and sells it for $3.00, the profit generated equals $2.00. In fact, this is not true. As a business operator, you must realise that the difference between what you have paid for the goods you sell and the price at which you sell them does not represent your actual profit. Instead, all expenses, including advertising, the building housing your operation, management salaries, and the labour required to generate the sale, to name but a few, are expenses that must be subtracted before you can determine your profits accurately.

Every foodservice operator is faced with the following profit-oriented formula:

Revenue - Expenses = Profit

Thus, when you manage your facility, you will receive revenue, the money you take in, and you will incur expenses, the cost of the items rquired to operate the business. The dollars that remain after all expenses have been paid represent your profit. For the purposes of this book, the authors will use the following terms interchangeably: revenues and sales; expenses and costs.

This formula holds even in the "nonprofit" sector of foodservice management. For example, consider the situation of Hector Bentevina. Hector is the foodservice manager at the headquarters of a large corporation. Hector supplies the foodservice to a large group of office workers, each of whom is employed by the corporation that owns the facility Hector manages. In this situation, Hector's employer clearly does not have "profit" as its primary motive. In most business dining situations, food is provided as a service to the company's employees either as a no-cost (to the employee) benefit or at a greatly reduced price. In some cases, executive dining rooms may be operated for the convenience of management. In all cases, however, some provision for profit must be made.

In your own operation, if you find that revenue is less than or equal to real expense, with no reserve for the future, you will likely also find that there is no money for new equipment; needed equipment maintenance may not be performed; employee raises (as well as your own) may be few and far between; and, in general, the foodservice facility will become outdated due to a lack of funds needed to remodel and upgrade. The truth is, all foodservice operations need revenue in excess of expenses if they are to thrive. If you manage a foodservice operation in a profit or a nonprofit setting, it will be your responsibility to communicate this message to your own staff.

Profit is the result of solid planning, sound management, and careful decision making. The purpose of this text is to give you the information and tools you need to make informed decisions with regard to managing your operation's revenue and expenses. If these tools are utilised properly, the potential for achieving profits you desire is greatly enhanced.

Profit should not be viewed as what is left over after the bills are paid. In fact, careful planning is necessary to earn a profit. In most cases, investors will not invest in businesses that do not generate enough profit to make their investment worthwhile. The restaurant business can be very profitable; however, there is no guarantee that an individual restaurant will in fact make a profit. Some restaurants do, while others do not. Because that is true, a more appropriate formula, which recognises and rewards the business owner for the risk associated with business ownership or investment, is as follows:

Revenue - Desired Profit = Ideal Expense

Ideal expense, in this case, is defined as management's view of the correct or appropriate amount of expense necessary to generate a given quantity of revenue. Desired profit is defined as the profit that the owner wants to achieve on that predicted quantity of revenue. This formula clearly places profit as a reward for providing service, not a leftover.

When foodservice managers deliver quality and value to their guests, anticipated revenue levels can be achieved and desired profit is attainable. Desired profit and ideal expense levels are not, however, easily achieved. It takes an astute foodservice operator to consistently make decisions that will maximise revenue while holding expenses to the ideal or appropriate amount.

Revenue

To some degree, you can manage your revenue levels. Revenue dollars are the result of units sold. These units may consist of individual menu items, lunches, dinners, drinks, or any other item produced by your operation. Revenue varies with both the number of guests frequenting your business and the amount of money spent by each guest. You can increase revenue by increasing the number of guests you serve, by increasing the amount each guest spends, or by a combination of both approaches.

Adding seating or drive-through windows, extending operating hours, and building additional foodservice units are all examples of management's efforts to increase the number of guests choosing to come to the restaurant or foodservice operation. Suggestive selling by service staff, creative menu pricing techniques, as well as discounts for very large purchases are all examples of efforts to increase the amount of money each guest spends.

It is the opinion of the authors that management's primary task is to take the steps necessary to bring guests to the foodservice operation. This is true because the profit formula begins with revenue. Experienced foodservice operators know that increasing revenue through adding guests, suggestive selling, or possibly raising menu prices is an extremely effective way of increasing overall profitability, but only if effective cost management systems are in place.

Marketing efforts, restaurant design and site selection, employee training and food preparation methods are all critical links in the revenue-producing chain. No amount of effective expense control can solve the profit problems caused by inadequate revenue resulting from inferior food quality or service levels. Effective cost control, however, when coupled with management's aggressive attitude toward meeting and exceeding guests' expectations, can result in outstanding revenue and profit performance.

Food Service Expenses

There are four major foodservice expense categories that you must learn to control. They are:

Food costs

Food costs are the costs associated with actually producing the menu items a guest selects. They include the expense of meats, dairy, fruits, vegetables, and other categories of food items produced by the foodservice operation. When computing food costs, many operators include the cost of minor paper and plastic items, such as the paper wrappers used to wrap sandwiches. In most cases, food costs will make up the largest or second largest expense category you must learn to manage.

Beverage costs

Beverage costs are those related to the sale of alcoholic beverages. It is interesting to note that it is common practice in the hospitality industry to consider beverage costs of a nonalcoholic nature as an expense in the food cost category. Thus, milk, tea, coffee, carbonated beverages, and other nonalcoholic beverage items are not generally considered a beverage cost. Alcoholic beverages accounted for in the beverage cost category include beer, wine, and liquor. This category may also include the costs of ingredients necessary to produce these drinks, such as cherries, lemons, olives, limes, mixers like carbonated beverages and juices, and other items commonly used in the production and service of alcoholic beverages.

Labour costs

Labour costs include the cost of all employees necessary to run the business. This expense category would also include the amount of any taxes you are required to pay when you have employees on your payroll. Some operators find it helpful to include the cost of management in this category. Others prefer to place the cost of managers in the category of other expenses. In most operations labour costs are an operator's highest cost, or they are second only to food costs in total dollars spent. If management is included as a labour cost, then this category will frequently be even larger than the food cost category.

Other expenses

Other expenses include all expenses that are neither food, nor beverage, nor labour. Examples include franchise fees, utilities, rent, linen, and such items as china, glassware, kitchen knives, and pots and pans. While this expense category is sometimes incorrectly referred to as "minor expenses," your ability to successfully control this expense area is especially critical to the overall profitability of your foodservice unit.

Percentage calculations are important for at least two major reasons. First and foremost, percentages are the most common standard used for evaluating costs in the foodservice industry. Therefore, knowledge of what a percent is and how it is calculated is vital. Second, as a manager in the foodservice industry, you will be evaluated primarily on your ability to compute, analyse, and control these percent figures. While it is true that many basic management tools such as Microsoft Excel, Lotus, and other software programmes will "compute" percentages for you, it is important that you understand what the percentages mean and how they should be interpreted. Percent calculations are used extensively in this text and are a cornerstone of any effective cost control system.

Percent review

Understanding percents and how they are mathematically computed is important. The following review may be helpful for some readers. If you thoroughly understand the percent concept, you may skip this section and the Computing Percent section and proceed directly to the Using Percent section. Percent (%) means "out of each hundred." Thus, 10 percent would mean 10 out of each 100. If we asked how many guests would buy blueberry pie on a given day, and the answer is 10 percent, then 10 people out of each 100 we serve will select blueberry pie. If 52 percent of your employees are female, then 52 out of each 100 employees are female. If 15 percent of your employees will receive a raise this month, then 15 out of 100 employees will get their raise.

Common form

In its common form, the % sign is used to express the percentage. If we say 10 percent, then we mean "10 out of each 100" and no further explanation is necessary. The common form, the percent, is equivalent to the same amount expressed in either the fraction or the decimal form.

Fraction form

In fraction form, the percent is expressed as the part, or a portion of 100. Thus, 10 percent is written as 10 "over" 100 (10/100). This is simply another way of expressing the relationship between the part (10) and the whole (100).

Decimal form

A decimal is a number developed from the counting system we use. It is based on the fact that we count to 10 then start over again. In other words, each of our major units, 10s, 100s, 1,000s, and so on, are based on the use of 10s, and each number can easily be divided by 10. Instead of using the % sign, the decimal form uses the (.) or decimal point to express the percent relationship. Thus, 10 percent is expressed as 0.10 in decimal form. The numbers to the right of the decimal point express the percentage.

Each of these three methods of expressing percentages is used in the foodservice industry, and to be successful you must develop a clear understanding of how a percentage is computed. Once that is known, you can express the percentage in any form that is required or that is useful to you.

Computing percent

To determine what percent one number is of another number, divide the number that is the part by the number that is the whole. Usually, but not always, this means dividing the smaller number by the larger number. For example, assume that 840 guests were served during a banquet at your hotel; 420 of them asked for coffee with their meal. To find what percent of your guests ordered coffee, divide the part (420) by the whole (840).

Thus, 50% (common form), 50/100 (fraction form), or 0.50 (decimal form) represents the proportion of people at the banquet who ordered coffee. A large number of new foodservice managers have difficulty computing percent figures. It is easy to forget which number goes "on the top" and which number goes "on the bottom." In general, if you attempt to compute a percentage and get a whole number (a number larger than 1), either a mistake has been made or costs are extremely high! Many people also become confused when converting from one form of percent to another. If that is a problem, remember the following conversion rules:

— To convert from common form to decimal form, move the decimal two places to the left, that is, 50.00% = 0.50.

— To convert from decimal form to common form, move the decimal two places to the right, that is, 0.40 = 40.00%.

In a restaurant, the "whole" is usually a revenue figure. Expenses and profits are the "parts," which are usually expressed in terms of a percent. It is interesting to note that, in the United States, the same system in use for our numbers is in use for our money. Each dime contains 10 pennies, each dollar contains 10 dimes, and so on. Thus when discussing money, it is true that a percent refers to "cents out of each dollar" as well as "out of each 100 dollars." When we say 10 percent of a dollar, we mean 10 cents, or "10 cents out of each dollar." Likewise, 25 percent of a dollar represents 25 cents, 50 percent of a dollar represents 50 cents, and 100 percent of a dollar represents $1.00.

Sometimes, when using percent to express the relationship between portions of a dollar and the whole, we find that the part is, indeed, larger than the whole. Great care must always be taken when computing percents, so that the percent arrived at is of help to you in your work and does not represent an error in mathematics.

Using percent

Consider a restaurant that you are operating. Imagine that your revenues for a week are in the amount of $1,600. Expenses for the same week are $1,200. Excess costs could account for the difference. If these costs could be identified and corrected, we could perhaps achieve the desired profit percentage. Most foodservice operators compute many cost percentages, not just one. The major cost divisions used in foodservice are as follows:

— Food and beverage cost

— Labour cost

— Other expense

A modified profit formula, therefore, looks as follows:

Revenue - (Food and Beverage Cost + Labour Cost + Other Expenses) = Profit

Understanding the Income (Profit and Loss) Statement

All of Pat's expenses and profits can be computed as percents by using the revenue figure, $400,000, as the whole, with expenses and profit representing the parts as on the following:

An accounting tool that details revenue, expenses, and profit for a given period of time, is called the income statement, which is commonly called the profit and-loss statement (P&L). It lists revenue, food and beverage cost, labour cost, and other expense. The P&L also identifies profits since, as you recall, profits are generated by the formula:

Revenue - Expense = Profit

The pieces of the pie represent Pat's cost and profit categories. Costs and profit total 100 percent, which is equal to Pat's total revenues. To put it in another way, out of every revenue dollar that Pat generates, 100 percent is designated as either costs or profit.

Pat knows from the P&L that revenues represent 100 percent of the total dollars available to cover expenses and provide for a profit. Food and beverage cost is 37.50 percent, and labour cost percentage in the steakhouse equals 43.75 percent. Other expense percentage equals 6.25 percent, and her total expense percent is 87.50 percent (37.50 + 43.75 + 6.25 = 87.50 percent). The steakhouse profit equals 12.50 percent. Thus, for each dollar in revenue, Pat earns a profit of 12.50 cents. Pat's revenue, expense, and profit information is contained in the steakhouse's P&L.

In restaurants that serve alcohol, food costs and beverage costs are most often separated into two categories in the P&L. Likewise, food revenues and beverage revenues are reported separately. This is done so that the food cost can be compared to food revenues, and the beverage cost can be compared to beverage revenues. Suppose, for example, that one manager is responsible for controlling food cost percent in the restaurant and another manager is responsible for controlling beverage cost percent in the bar. Separation of these two "departments," then, is especially helpful when evaluating the performance of these two managers. It also helps these managers to quickly identify and anticipate problems associated with their costs and identify ways to correct these problems.

The P&L is important because it indicates the efficiency and profitability of an operation. Because so many individuals and groups are interested in a food facility's performance, it is important that the P&L and other financial statements are prepared in a manner that is consistent with other facilities. If, for example, you own two Italian restaurants, it would be very confusing if one of your managers used a particular method for preparing his or her unit's P&L, while the other manager used an entirely different method. You, your investors, your accountant, governmental taxing entities, and your creditors may all be interested in your operational results, and unless you report and account for these in a manner they can easily understand, confusion may result.

To avoid such a set of circumstances, the Uniform System of Accounts is used to report financial results in most foodservice units. This system was created to ensure uniform reporting of financial results. A Uniform System of Accounts exists for restaurants, another for hotels, and another for clubs. The Uniform System of Accounts will be discussed in greater detail later in this text.

The primary purpose of preparing a P&L is to identify revenue, expenses, and profits for a given time period. As a manager, your efforts, more than any other factor, will influence your operation's profitability. Good managers provide excellent value to their guests, which cause guests to return, and thus increases revenue. In addition, good managers know how to analyse, manage, and control their costs. For these managers, expenses are held to the amount that was preplanned.

The result is the desired profit level. Good managers influence the success of their units and their own employees. The results for them personally are promotions, added responsibilities, and salary increases. If you wish to succeed in the hospitality industry, it is important to remember that your performance will be evaluated primarily on your ability to achieve the profit levels your operation has planned for. In addition to your own efforts, many factors influence profit dollars and profit percent, and you must be aware, and in control, of all of them.

Understanding the Budget

Some foodservice managers do not generate revenue on a

daily basis. Consider, for a moment, the foodservice manager at a summer camp run for children. In this case, parents pay a fixed fee to cover housing, activities, and meals for a set period of time. The foodservice director, in this situation, is just one of several managers who must share this revenue. If too many dollars are spent on providing housing or play activities, too few dollars may be available to provide an adequate quantity or quality of meals. On the other hand, if too many dollars are spent on providing foodservice, there may not be enough left to cover other needed expense areas.

In a case like this, foodservice operators should prepare a budget. A budget is simply an estimate of projected revenue, expense, and profit. In some hospitality companies, the budget is known as the plan, referring to the fact that the budget details the operation's estimated, or "planned for," revenue and expense for a given accounting period. An accounting period is an hour, day, week, or month in which an operator wishes to analyse revenue and expenses. All effective managers, whether in the commercial (for profit) or nonprofit sector, use budgets. Budgeting is simply planning for revenue, expense, and profit. If these items are planned for, you can determine how close your actual performance is to your plan or budget. In the summer camp example, the following information is known:

— Number of campers: 180

— Number of meals served to each camper per day: 3

— Length of campers' stay: 7 days

With 180 campers eating 3 meals each day for 7 days, 3,780 meals will be served. Generally, in a case such as the summer camp, the foodservice director is given a dollar amount that represents the allowed expense for each meal to be served. For example, if $1.85 per meal is the amount budgeted for this director, the total revenue budget would equal $6,993. From this figure, an expense budget can begin to be developed. In this case, we are interested in the amount of expenses budgeted and the amount actually spent on expenses. Equally important, we would be interested in the percent of the budget actually used, a concept known as performance to budget.

A simple example may help to firmly establish the idea of budget and performance to budget. Assume that a child has $1.00 per day to spend on candy. On Monday morning, the child's parents give the child $1.00 for each day of the week, or $7.00 total. If the child spends only $ 1.00 per day, he or she will be able to buy candy all week. If, however, too much is spent in any one day, there may not be any money left at the end of the week.

Many foodservice operations are changing from "one month" budget periods to periods of 28 days. The 28-day-period approach divides a year into 13 equal periods of 28 days each. Therefore, each period has four Mondays, four Tuesdays, four Wednesdays, and so on. This helps the manager compare performance from one period to the next without having to compensate for "extra days" in any one period. The downside of this approach is that you can no longer talk about the month of March, for example, because "period 3" would occur during part of February and part of March. Although using the 28-day-period approach takes a while to get used to, it is an effective way to measure performance and plan from period to period.

Many operators use the concept of "significant" variation to determine whether a cost control problem exists. In this case, a significant variation is any variation in expected costs that management feels is an area of concern. This variation can be caused by costs that were either higher or lower than the amount originally budgeted or planned for.

When you manage a foodservice operation and you find that significant variations from your planned results occur, you must:

— Identify the problem.

— Determine the cause.

— Take corrective action.

It is crucial to know the kind of problem you have if you are to be an effective problem solver. Management's attention must be focused on the proper place. In this case, the proper areas for concern are other expense and profit. If, in the future, food expense became too low, it, too, would be an area of concern. Why? Remember that expenses create revenue; thus, it is not your goal to eliminate expense.

In fact, those managers who focus too much on eliminating expense, instead of building revenue, often find that their expenses are completely eliminated when they are forced to close their operation's doors permanently because guests did not feel they received good value for the money spent at that restaurant! Control and management of revenue and expense are important. Elimination of either is not desired. As you have seen, revenue and expense directly impact profit. Your important role as a hospitality manager is to analyse, manage, and control your costs so that you achieve planned results. It can be done, and it can be fun.

Bibliography

Bradley, Alice, *Cooking for profit; catering and food service management,* Chicago: American school of home economics, 1922.)

Dahl, J. O., *200 ways to control food costs in quantity cookery,* Stamford Conn: The Dahls, 1941.

______________ ., *Dictionary of 1001 menu terms, foods, wines, spirits, cocktails,* Stamford Conn: J.O. Dahl, 1936.

______________ . and J. H. Breland, *Food standards handbook for quantity cookery,* Stamford Conn: Whitlock Press, 1945.

Fellows, Charles, *Fellows' menu maker; suggestions for selecting and arranging menus for hotels and* restaurants, with object of changing from day to day to give continuous variety of foods in season, Chicago: The Hotel monthly, 1910.

Frooman, Abraham Arthur, *Five steps to effective institutional food buying, by A. A. Frooman,* Chicago, 1948.

Gray, Madeline and Vass De Lo Padua, *How to cook for profit; a complete guide to food in quantity, from order pad to diner's table.* New York: Greenberg, 1947.

Horwath, Ernest B. and Louis Toth, *Hotel accounting, including departmental control, food costing, and auditing,* New York: The Ronald press company, 1928.

Livingstone, Helen, *Food service; for restaurant, coffee shop, hotel, cafeteria, home,* Blooming Ill: McKnight and McKnight Pub. Co., 1950.

Searing, Fred, *Profit building ideas for food and food service,* Stanford, Conn.: Dahl Pub. Co., 1947.

Vehling, Joseph Dommers et al. *Cooking, or, Practical and economical training for those who are to be* servants, wives, and mothers: management of the kitchen, plain cooking, bread-making, baking, brewing, *pickling, etc.* London: J. Masters, 1854.

Wadhams, Caroline Reed, *Simple directions for the waitress or parlor maid,* New York: Longmans Green and co., 1917.

Walsh, Joseph F., *Sound spending, with special reference to the operating cost of institutions, schools, colleges, hospitals, orphanages, convents, monasteries, etc., seminaries, parishes,* Cleveland: Seminary press, 1935.

Wenzel, G. L., *Handbook of restaurant costs: how to maintain a 40% food cost and a 25% payroll,* Austin, Texas: G. Wenzel?, 1948.

West, Bessie Brooks and LeVelle Wood, *Food service in institutions,* New York; London: J. Wiley & sons inc; Chapman & Hall limited, 1938.

Whitehead, Jessup, *The steward's handbook and guide to party catering,* Chicago: J. Anderson & co. printers, 1889.

Index